NATURAL SOAP MAKING

150 Unique Beauty Soap, Medicated Soap, Glycerin Soap, Liquid Soap, Goat Milk Soap & So Much More

TABLE OF CONTENTS
Introduction

Cold Process Soap Recipes
Floral Scented Soaps
- #1 Rose Swirls
- #2 Pure Baby's Breath
- #3 Swirling Wild Rose
- #4 Orchid Swirls
- #5 Daisy Print
- #6 Violet Sprinkles
- #7 Geranium and Violet
- #8 Lavender and Hops
- #9 Sunshine Calendula
- #10 Floral Garden Soap

Unique Soaps
- #1 Pink Gold Soap
- #2 Milk and Clay Soap

- #3 Jade Swirl
- #4 Eggnog Soap
- #5 Simple Black Tea
- #6 Energizing Coffee
- #7 Simple Orange Zest
- #8 Amber and Evergreen Soap
- #9 Honey Soap
- #10 Nettle, Spearmint & Lime

Medicated Soap Recipes
- #1 Soothing Aloe Vera Soap
- #2 Charcoal and Bamboo Soap
- #3 Tea Tree Oil Soap
- #4 Insecticidal Soap
- #5 Lavender and Peppermint Antiseptic Soap
- #6 Soothing Chamomile Soap
- #7 Skin Blemish Soap
- #8 Acne Fighter
- #9 Baking Soda and Oatmeal Skin Bar
- #10 Yogurt Soap

Hot Process Soap Recipes
Floral Scented Soap Recipes
- #1 Frankincense Soap
- #2 Rosemary Mint Soap
- #3 Calendula Summer Soap
- #4 Lavender Soap
- #5 Honey and Chamomile Soap
- #6 Beautiful Rose Soap
- #7 Lilac Swirl
- #8 Dandelion Soap
- #9 Lavender Rosemary Soap
- #10 Eucalyptus and Lavender Soap

Unique Soaps
- #1 Icy Blue Soap
- #2 Irish Rain
- #3 Fruit Clay Bar
- #4 Spiced Apple Soap
- #5 Vanilla Latte Soap
- #5 Warm Cider Soap

- #7 Orange Spice Soap
- #8 Honey Vanilla Soap
- #9 Cranberry Soap
- #10 Pine and Peppermint

Medicated Soap Recipes
- #1 Skin Lotion Bar
- #2 Avocado Hair Rescue Bars
- #3 Calming Chamomile Soap
- #4 Acne Fighter with Tea Tree and Orange
- #5 Cellulite Eraser
- #6 Dry Skin Relief
- #7 Soothing Aloe Vera
- #8 Bastille Honey Skin Soap
- #9 Rose Infused Balancing Soap
- #10 Sensitive Skin Bar

Melt and Pour Soap Recipes
Floral Scented Soaps
- #1 Rose Soap
- #2 Lavender Honey Soap
- #3 Square Carnations
- #4 Rose Petal Soap
- #5 Jasmine Citrus Soap
- #6 Lilac Soap
- #7 Lemongrass and Green Tea
- #8 Sea Salt Jasmine
- #9 Floral Garden Bar
- #10 Sunrise Garden Bar

Unique Soaps
- #1 Lemon Poppy Seed
- #2 Candy Corn Soap
- #3 Honey Vanilla with Oatmeal
- #4 Pumpkin Spice Bars
- #5 Peaches and Cream Soap
- #6 Ground Coffee Soap
- #7 Cinnamon Oatmeal Soap
- #8 Vanilla Cinnamon Soap
- #9 Citrus Soap
- #10 Tropical Soap

Medicated Soaps
- #1 Lavender and Oatmeal Soother
- #2 Turmeric Soap
- #3 Pure Charcoal Soap
- #4 Coffee and Cream Soap
- #5 Citrus Antibacterial Soap
- #6 Chest Decongestant
- #7 Soothing Oatmeal Soap
- #8 Triple Butter, Charcoal and Clay Bar
- #9 Cucumber, Avocado, and Oats
- #10 Charcoal and Peppermint

Glycerin, Liquid & Goat Milk Soaps

Glycerin Soap Recipes
- #1 Apple Soap
- #2 Apricot Soap
- #3 Candy Cane Soap
- #4 Cherry Cheesecake
- #5 Chocolate Soap
- #6 Citronella Soap
- #7 Coffee and Cream
- #8 Rosemary and Cream
- #9 Cinnamon Soap
- #10 Aloe Vera and Nettle

Liquid Soap Recipes
- #1 Liquid Castile Soap
- #2 Liquid Dish Soap
- #3 Moisturizing Cream Hand Soap
- #4 Liquid Body Wash
- #5 Foaming Liquid Soap
- #6 Charcoal Facial Cleanser
- #7 Honey and Dandelion Floral Liquid Soap
- #8 Lavender and Oatmeal Body Wash
- #9 Moisturizing Soap
- #10 Liquid Laundry Soap

Goat Milk Soap
- The Process
  - #1 Oatmeal and Honey
  - #2 Rosemary and Peppermint

#3 Avocado and Dill
#4 Milk and Honey
#5 Rosemary
#6 Cinnamon
#7 Tropical Fruit
#8 Thyme
#9 Frankincense and Lavender
#10 Basic Goat Milk

Last Words

COLD PROCESS SOAP RECIPES

FLORAL SCENTED SOAPS

#1 Rose Swirls

This soap combines a beautiful modern scent with a classic design. The classic swirl design is made through a technique called an in-the-pot swirl. It is a simple process that allows each bar of soap to look unique.

Ingredients:

- ☐ 10-inch Silicone Loaf Mold
- ☐ 33 ounces of preferred cold process soap mix or quick mix
- ☐ 4.7 ounces of Sodium Hydroxide Lye
- ☐ 10.9 ounces of distilled water
- ☐ 2 teaspoons Sodium Lactate
- ☐ 2 ounces Wild Rose Fragrance Oil
- ☐ ½ teaspoon Rose Pearl Mica
- ☐ Pink Rose Petals

Directions:

1. Prepare the lye as we discussed in the previous book.
2. Prepare your oils by melting the 33 ounces of oil mix and setting aside until it reaches 110 to 130 degrees Fahrenheit.
3. Prepare your scent by weighing out the Wild Rose Fragrance Oil in a small glass cup.
4. Slowly combine the lye solution to the oil mixture. Pulse the blender on and off for about a minute. The soap should be at the texture of thin pudding.

5. Pour half of the soap in a separate container. Add the Rose Pearl Mica to one container and use a whisk to mix the color in thoroughly.
6. Add the fragrance oil evenly into both container and use a whisk to mix thoroughly.
7. Pour dollops of the white soap mix into the color soap mix in different areas and at different heights. Use a spoon and stir the soap two to three times in order to create more swirls, but make sure you don't overmix.
8. Pour the batter into your final mold and tap firmly to release bubbles. Allow the soap to sit for two to three minutes and then create texture on the top of the soap with a spoon.
9. Sprinkle the rose petals on the top of the soap.
10. Place the soap in a warm, room-temperature area and allow to harden for two to three days.
11. Once ready, remove the soap from the mold and lay it on its side to cut into bars.
12. Allow the bars to cure on a well-ventilated shelf for four to six weeks.

#2 Pure Baby's Breath

Baby's breath are very delicate flowers, and a soap based on their scent is very simple and pure.

Ingredients:

- ☐ Loaf Mold
- ☐ 6.8 ounces Canola Oil
- ☐ 1.2 ounces Castor Oil
- ☐ 10 ounces Coconut Oil
- ☐ 8 ounces Palm Oil
- ☐ 6 ounces Shea Oil

- ☐ 8 ounces Sweet Almond Oil
- ☐ 5.6 ounces Sodium Hydroxide Lye
- ☐ 11.2 ounces Distilled Water
- ☐ 2.5 ounces Baby's Breath Fragrance Oil
- ☐ 2 teaspoons Titanium Dioxide
- ☐ Dried Baby's Breath Flowers

Directions:

1. Add 5.6 ounces of lye slowly and carefully to 11.2 ounces of water and stir until the lye is completely dissolved and the liquid is clear. Set aside to cool.
2. In a second large glass bowl, combine all the oils and melt them completely.
3. Add the Titanium Dioxide to the oils and use a stick blender to combine until the chunks are gone.
4. Once both the lye and oil have cooled to 100 to 110 degrees Fahrenheit, you can combine them with a stick blender until a thin trace.
5. Add in the Baby's Breath Fragrance Oil and mix with the stick blender until you reach a medium trace.
6. Pour the soap mix into the mold and firmly tap to remove bubbles. Use a spoon to create a very light texture on the top.
7. Sprinkle the dried Baby's Breath on top, then wear gloves while gently pressing the flowers into the soap, so they stick.
8. Spritz the top with 99% isopropyl alcohol in order to prevent soda ash.
9. Place the soap in the freezer for 24 hours to prevent cracking and glycerin rivers.
10. Once the soap is fully thawed, allow it to harden for an additional two to three days.

11. Remove from the mold, lay it on its side and cut into bars.
12. Allow the bars to cure for four to six weeks.

#3 Swirling Wild Rose

This soap offers you a slightly stronger rose scent but can be a bit challenging to get the right balance for those new to making swirled soaps.

Ingredients:

- [ ] 18 bar mold with liner
- [ ] 2 ounces Castor Oil
- [ ] 16.3 ounces Coconut Oil
- [ ] 20.8 ounces Olive Oil
- [ ] 13 ounces Palm Oil
- [ ] 6.5 ounces Sunflower Oil
- [ ] 6.5 ounces Sweet Almond Oil
- [ ] 9.1 ounces Sodium Hydroxide Lye
- [ ] 21.5 ounces Distilled Water
- [ ] 4 ounces Wild Rose Fragrance Oil
- [ ] 1 teaspoon Rose Pearl Mica
- [ ] 1 teaspoon Shamrock Green Mica
- [ ] 2 teaspoons Titanium Dioxide
- [ ] Pink Rose Petals

Directions:

1. Start by preparing your colors. Place the Titanium dioxide into 2 tablespoons of a liquid oil of your choice. Use a hand mixer to get rid of all clumps. In separate containers you want to mix the Shamrock Green and Rose Pearl Mica; each mixed with 1 tablespoon of any lightweight

liquid oil and mixed until there are no clumps.
2. Add 9.1 ounces of lye to 21.5 ounces of water slowly and carefully, gently stir until the lye is completely dissolved and the liquid is clear. Set aside to cool.
3. Combine the oils and melt. Once the oils, as well as the lye, have cooled to 130 degrees Fahrenheit, then you can combine them and stick blend them to a very thin trace.
4. Divide the soap into four equal containers of about 700 milliliters. Add the following colors per container and whisk until completely incorporated.
    a. 1 tablespoon titanium dioxide for a white color.
    b. 1 teaspoon titanium dioxide with ½ teaspoon Rose Pearl Mica for a light pink color.
    c. 2 teaspoons of Rose Pearl Mica for a pink color.
    d. 1 teaspoon of Shamrock Green Mica for a green color.
5. Divide the fragrance equally between the containers and whisk to mix completely.
6. Pour any of the colors into the mold first in long S-curves lengthwise.
7. Pour any second color into the mold, still with long lengthwise S-curves.
8. Continue doing this with alternate colors.
9. As the mold gets halfway full, be careful to make sure you differentiate the colors to have a more distinct pattern.
10. Once you are at the top of the mold, you want to pour so that each color is visible.
11. After all the soap is in the mold, tap it firmly to remove air bubbles.
12. Use a chopstick, dowel or other wood stick and drag to cross the lines you created with the soap. Make this S-curve pattern throughout the soap until you've swirled the entire mold.
13. Insert the dividers in the mold, so they reach the bottom in all sections, or you can wait and cut your bars later.

14. Sprinkle pink rose petals in a pattern you desire on each bar and gently press into the soap with a gloved hand.
15. Spritz the top of the some with 995 isopropyl alcohol in order to prevent soda ash.
16. Cover the mold and if needed place it on a heating pad for 30 minutes at medium heat.
17. Keep the soap in the mold for two to three days and then remove from the mold once firm enough to handle.
18. Allow the soap to cure for four to six weeks.

#4 Orchid Swirls

Orchids are a very sophisticated and regal flower with a beautiful scent that is worth capturing in soap. Orchid Fragrance Oil is a complex mix of flowers, balsam, and musk. Along with the sophisticated smell you want a regal appearance with a rich color.

Ingredients:

- ☐ Loaf Mold
- ☐ 33 ounces desired soap oil mix or quick mix
- ☐ 4.7 ounces Sodium Hydroxide Lye
- ☐ 10.9 ounces Distilled Water
- ☐ 1.5 ounces Orchid Fragrance Oil
- ☐ 1 teaspoon Titanium Dioxide
- ☐ 1 teaspoon Purple Mica
- ☐ ½ teaspoon Activated Charcoal
- ☐ Dried Jasmine Flowers

Directions:

1. Prepare your colors by making three bowls; one for each color. The titanium dioxide and purple mica should be mixed with one tablespoon of your desired liquid oil and mixed until there are no clumps. The activated charcoal should be mixed with a ½ tablespoon of a lightweight liquid oil.
2. Add 4.7 ounces of lye to 10.9 ounces of water slowly and carefully; gently mixing under the lye is completely dissolved and the liquid is clear. Set aside to cool.
3. Melt the desired oils or the quick mix until clear.
4. After the lye and oils have cooled to 130 degrees Fahrenheit or lower, combine them and stick blend until you reach a thin trace.
5. Pour off about 400 ml of the soap mix into a separate container.
6. In the larger container, add the purple mica. Add about 1/16 teaspoon of the activated charcoal mix if you want a deeper and richer color. Mix the color completely with a whisk.
7. To the small soap container add the titanium dioxide and mix completely with a whisk.
8. Add the Orchid Fragrance Oil evenly to both soap containers and mix completely with a whisk.
9. Make sure you have a medium trace, otherwise pulse with the stick blender until you are at the right trace. Take care not to over blend the soap.
10. After you reach a medium trace, pour the white soap into the purple soap in different areas. It is best to pour from a high point, so the soap reaches the entire depth of the bowl.
11. After all the white soap is added, use a spatula or large spoon to swirl both colors. About two to three times is usually sufficient without muddling the colors.
12. Pour the soap into the mold and tap firmly to remove bubbles.

13. Create peaks in the top of the soap with a spoon, if it is too thin wait about two to three minutes.
14. Sprinkle the dried jasmine flowers on the top and gently press into the soap with a gloved hand.
15. Spritz the top with 99% isopropyl alcohol to prevent soda ash.
16. Lightly insulate the soap by placing in a drawer in a room that stays about seventy degrees Fahrenheit.
17. Let the soap sit for two to three days.
18. Remove the soap from the mold and cut into bars.
19. Let the bars cure for four to six weeks.

#5 Daisy Print

Daisies are a cheerful flower, and this soap will bring up images of a perfect spring day. This recipe takes a little more time since you have to make some embeds a few days in advance before making the final soap.

Ingredients:

Embeds:
- [ ] 3 mini daisy silicone column molds
- [ ] 2.8 ounces Coconut Oil
- [ ] 3.3 ounces Olive Oil
- [ ] 2.8 ounces Palm Oil
- [ ] 2.2 ounces Sunflower Oil
- [ ] 1.6 ounces Sodium Hydroxide Lye
- [ ] 3.6 ounces Distilled Water
- [ ] 2 teaspoons Titanium Dioxide

Base:

- ☐ Loaf Mold
- ☐ 8 ounces Coconut Oil
- ☐ 9.6 ounces Olive Oil
- ☐ 8 ounces Palm Oil
- ☐ 6.4 ounces Sunflower Oil
- ☐ 4.6 ounces Sodium Hydroxide Lye
- ☐ 10.6 ounces Distilled Water
- ☐ 2.5 ounces Sunflower Fragrance Oil
- ☐ ½ teaspoon Yellow Oxide
- ☐ 1 teaspoon Titanium Dioxide

Directions:

Embeds:
1. Start making the embeds at least three to four days in advance of the main soap.
2. Mix 2 teaspoons titanium dioxide in 1 tablespoon liquid oil of your choice.
3. Combine the lye and water slowly and carefully, gently stirring until it is fully dissolved and clear. Set aside to cool.
4. Place the embeds into a tall, stable container where they will be able to stand vertically.
5. Combine all the oils and fully melt them.
6. Once the oils and lye have cooled to 130 degrees Fahrenheit or less, then you can combine them and stick blend to a thin trace.
7. Add the titanium dioxide to the soap and whisk until fully mixed.
8. If the mixture is still thin, you can pulse it with the stick blender until you have a medium trace.
9. Carefully pour the soap into the molds until full. Set the molds aside

someplace secure where they won't get spilled.
10. In three days you can test and see if the molds pull apart easily. If they don't, give them another day or two.
11. Once you are able to remove them from the molds, cut them to fit lengthwise in the loaf mold for the main soap.

Main Soap:
1. Prepare the color in two separate containers. In one combine the titanium dioxide with 1 tablespoon of a liquid oil of your choice and whisk until fully combined. In the other container, combine the yellow oxide with ½ tablespoon lightweight liquid oil of your choice and whisk until fully combined. Use a mini mixer if needed to avoid any clumps.
2. Add the lye and water slowly and carefully, gently stirring until it is fully dissolved and the liquid is clear. Set aside to allow to cool.
3. Combine and completely melt the oils.
4. After the lye and oil have cooled to 130 degrees Fahrenheit or less, combine them and stick blend until you have a thin trace.
5. Add the yellow oxide and titanium dioxide, whisk until completely mixed.
6. Add the Sunflower Fragrance Oil and whisk until completely mixed.
7. Test you trace since the soap needs to be at a medium trace in order to suspend the embeds. When you pull out the stick blender or whisk, you should see a defined trail on the top of the soap.
8. Pour a small amount of soap into the mold and completely cover the bottom.
9. Place one embed into the mold in the desired spot.
10. Gently cover the embed with more soap and continue to pour until half full.
11. Place the second embed into the mold in the desired spot and gently press in the place, then gently cover the embed with soap.

12. Pour soap into the mold until almost full.
13. Place your last embed in the desired spot and gently push in place.
14. Fill the mold with the remaining soap and tap to remove the air bubbles. Use a spoon to even the top.
15. Spritz the top with 99% isopropyl alcohol to prevent soda ash.
16. If you are in a hot area, you should place the soap in the refrigerator for three to four hours, especially if you are using a wooden mold in order to prevent cracking. Otherwise, you can leave the soap at room temperature. If you aren't sure, keep an eye on the soap for an hour or two and move it to the refrigerator if you notice any cracks developing on top.
17. Keep the soap in the mold for two to three days.
18. Remove from the mold and cut into bars.
19. Allow the bars to cure for four to six weeks.

#6 Violet Sprinkles

This soap has a sophisticated, yet playful appearance; with a rich and beautiful color. The sprinkles are also an excellent way to use an extra soap batch or a batch that didn't come out just right.

Ingredients:

- ☐ Loaf Mold
- ☐ 5-6 ounces of shredded soap
- ☐ 33 ounces of desired oil mix or quick mix
- ☐ 4.7 ounces Sodium Hydroxide Lye
- ☐ 10.8 ounces Distilled Water
- ☐ 2 ounces Violet Fragrance Oil

- ☐ ½ teaspoon titanium dioxide
- ☐ 2 teaspoons Purple Mica
- ☐ Lavender Mica

Directions:

1. Start by making your colors. In one container mix the titanium dioxide with ½ tablespoon liquid oil of your choice. In a second container, mix the purple mica with a lightweight liquid oil of your choice. If needed use a mini mixer to get rid of all clumps.
2. Shred some leftover soap scraps with a cheese grater. They don't have to be purple, they can be whatever you want for the finished soap. Set aside for later.
3. Add the lye to the water carefully and slowly; gently stir until fully dissolve and clear. Set aside to let cool.
4. Completely melt your choice oils or quick mix until it is clear.
5. Once both mixes are cooled to 130 degrees Fahrenheit or less, then you can combine them and stick blend until you have a light trace.
6. Divide the mixture into two separate containers: one should have about two cups while the other should be about four cups.
7. To the four cups add all the purple mica and whisk to mix fully.
8. Split the purple soap into two more batches of about two cups each.
9. To the uncolored soap, add the titanium dioxide and whisk to full mix.
10. To one of the purple soaps, add about ⅓ of the Violet Fragrance Oil and whisk to mix completely. Pulse with the stick blender if needed until it is a medium to thick trace.
11. Pour the scented soap into the mold and tap to release bubbles. Use a spatula or spoon to make divots and peaks in the soap.
12. To the white soap, add about ⅓ of the Violet Fragrance Oil and whisk to mix completely. Use a stick blender if needed until the mixture is

thickened. Add the shaved soap and whisk to mix evenly.
13. Pour the white soap on top of the scented purple mix. If the soap is thick, you may need to spoon it into the mold to evenly distribute it. If you can create peaks and divots in this layer as well.
14. Add the last of the Violet Fragrance Oil to the last purple soap and whisk to mix completely. If needed use the stick blender until thickened.
15. Drop the purple soap onto the two previous layers and use the spoon to even out the soap and create some texture. Just go for a look that you prefer.
16. Sprinkle lavender mica on the top as desired.
17. Spritz the soap with 99% isopropyl alcohol to prevent soda ash.
18. Leave the soap for two to three days.
19. Remove from the mold and cut into bars.
20. Allow curing for four to six weeks.

#7 GERANIUM AND VIOLET

This soap combines the delicate floral scent of two beautiful flowers. It is a simple and straightforward recipe for those who want to get a batch done quickly.

Ingredients:

- ☐ 5 ounces Apricot Kernel Oil
- ☐ 9 ounces Avocado Oil
- ☐ 2.5 ounces Cocoa Butter
- ☐ 5 ounces Coconut Oil
- ☐ 3.5 ounces Palm Oil
- ☐ 10 ounces Sweet Almond Oil
- ☐ 10 ounces Sunflower Seed Oil

- ☐ 13 ounces Distilled Water
- ☐ 6.2 ounces Sodium Hydroxide Lye
- ☐ 1 ounce Violet Fragrance Oil
- ☐ 1-ounce Geranium Fragrance Oil
- ☐ 2 teaspoon Alkanet root powder

Directions:

1. Blend the Alkanet with two teaspoons of water and use a mini mixer or a stick blender to remove the clumps.
2. Add the lye to the water slowly and carefully, gently blending until completely dissolved and clear. Set aside to cool.
3. Completely melt and blend the oils.
4. Once both the oils and the lye mixture are cooled to about 100 degrees Fahrenheit, you can combine them and use a stick blender to get it to a thin trace.
5. Add the fragrances and pink color to the soap and blend well.
6. Pour the soap into your desired shape mold.
7. If desired, texture the top of the soap.
8. Allow the soap to set for 24 hours.
9. Remove the soap and cut into bars.
10. Allow the bars to cure for four to six weeks.

#8 Lavender and Hops

This is a secret blend that gives you a truly unique bar of soap. It gives you a great lather without drying out your skin but also helps exfoliate. Plus the lovely lavender scent helps relax you.

Ingredients:

- ☐ 1 ounce Castor Oil
- ☐ 2 ounces Coconut Oil
- ☐ 2 ounces Palm Kernel Oil
- ☐ 4 ounces Olive Oil
- ☐ 4 ounces Lard
- ☐ 3 ounces Cocoa Butter
- ☐ 2.2-ounce Sodium Hydroxide Lye
- ☐ 6.08 ounces Distilled Water
- ☐ 0.5-ounce lavender and hops essential oil blend
- ☐ 2 teaspoon activated charcoal
- ☐ ½ teaspoon sea salt

Directions:

1. Add the lye to the water slowly and carefully, gently mixing until fully dissolved and clear.
2. Add the activated charcoal to the mixture and stir until completely mixed.
3. Strain the mixture as you add in all the oils.
4. At trace, add in the sea salt to give a starry effect.
5. Add your fragrance and mix until fully incorporated.
6. Pour into your desired mold and allow to set for 24 hours or until easy to remove from the mold.
7. Cut into bars and allow to cure for four to six weeks.

#9 SUNSHINE CALENDULA

This is a very refreshing and bright soap that is wonderful to use when you want to wake up and feel fresh in the morning. It is a simple and quick recipe that shouldn't take you long to make.

Ingredients:

- ☐ 6.9 ounces water
- ☐ 3.4 ounces Aloe Vera juice
- ☐ 4.4 ounces Sodium Hydroxide Lye
- ☐ 11 ounces Olive Oil
- ☐ 10.5 ounces Coconut Oil
- ☐ 7 ounces Rice Bran Oil
- ☐ 1.5 ounces Shea Butter
- ☐ 1.5 ounces Mango Butter
- ☐ 2 ounces Breezes and Sunshine Fragrance Oil
- ☐ 3 Tablespoons dried Calendula Petals
- ☐ 1 teaspoon yellow clay

Directions:

1. Add lye and water carefully and slowly until liquid is clear and lye is fully dissolved.
2. Add Aloe Vera juice and stir until completely mixed.
3. Melt oil together.
4. Combine lye and oils when cooled and mix well.
5. At trace, add your fragrance oil, 2 tablespoons Calendula Petals and yellow clay. Mixing until completely incorporated.
6. Pour into your mold and add 1 tablespoon of Calendula Petals to the top.
7. Allow to set for 24 hours or until you are easily able to remove from the mold.
8. Cut into bars and allow to cure for four to six weeks.

#10 FLORAL GARDEN SOAP

If you want a floral soap that stands out from all the rest, then give this recipe a try. It will give you the refreshing and beautiful scent of an entire flower garden.

Ingredients:

- ☐ 6.7 ounces High Oleic Sunflower Oil infused with calendula, lavender and chamomile buds and petals.
- ☐ 3.2 ounces Coconut Oil
- ☐ 3.04 ounces Babassu Oil
- ☐ 1.12 ounces Shea Butter
- ☐ 1.12 ounces Rosehip Oil
- ☐ 0.8 ounces Evening Primrose Oil
- ☐ 0.5 to 0.7 ounces rose and jasmine essential oils
- ☐ 6.08 ounces distilled water
- ☐ 2.3 ounces Sodium Hydroxide Lye

Directions:

1. Mix water and lye slowly and carefully until liquid is clear and lye is fully dissolved.
2. Melt oils until completely blended.
3. Combine oils and lye when cooled.
4. At trace, add essential oils.
5. Pour in your desired mold, cover and allow to set for 24 to 48 hours.
6. Remove from mold and cut into bars then cure for four to six weeks.

UNIQUE SOAPS

#1 Pink Gold Soap

Pink and gold make a very sophisticated color combination and is good for nearly any time of the year. Using a Rose Quartz Fragrance Oil with this color combination gives the soap a unique scent combination of many flowers including traditional rose, jasmine, and grapefruit.

Ingredients:

- ☐ Loaf Mold
- ☐ 1.8 ounces Cocoa Butter
- ☐ 11.6 ounces Coconut Oil
- ☐ 3.2 ounces Meadow foam Oil
- ☐ 11.6 ounces Palm Oil
- ☐ 7 ounces Rice Bran Oil
- ☐ 5 ounces Sodium Hydroxide Lye
- ☐ 10 ounces distilled water
- ☐ 1.75 ounces Rose Quartz Fragrance Oil
- ☐ 4 teaspoons Titanium Dioxide
- ☐ ⅓ teaspoon Magenta Mica
- ☐ Gold Sparkle Mica
- ☐ Pink Sea Salt

Directions:

1. Prepare your colors by mixing the Titanium Dioxide with 4 tablespoons

of your desired liquid oil until there are no clumps. In the second container mix the Magenta Mica with ½ tablespoon of a lightweight liquid oil until there are no clumps.
2. Gently, slowly and carefully stir together the water and lye until the liquid is clear and the lye is fully dissolved.
3. Combine and melt all your oils in a separate large bowl.
4. Add all of the Titanium Dioxide and use a stick blender to completely mix so you can remove all chunks without thickening the trace.
5. After cooling, you can combine the oils and lye and stick blend until you have a very thin trace.
6. Pour 600 ml of the soap into a separate container.
7. Add 1 teaspoon of the Magenta Mica into the smaller container of soap and whisk until mixed completely.
8. Add the Rose Quartz Fragrance Oil proportionally to both soap containers and whisk to mix thoroughly.
9. Make sure the pink soap is blended into a medium to thick trace.
10. Pour the pink soap into the mold and tap to remove air bubbles.
11. Sprinkle a layer of the Gold Sparkle Mica on the top, covering as much of the pink soap as possible; but don't put it on too thick otherwise the soap my separate when cut.
12. By now the white soap should be thicker. Use a spoon to drop small amounts of white soap on top until it completely covers the pink soap. Gently transfer the remaining white soap into the mold. Firmly tap the mold to help it settle and get rid of air bubbles.
13. Create texture on top with a small spoon.
14. Sprinkle more Gold Sparkle Mica on the top.
15. Sprinkle the pink sea salt on the top.
16. Spritz with 99% isopropyl alcohol to prevent soda ash.
17. Lightly insulate the soap by placing in a large draw uncovered and kept at room temperature. Allow to set for two to three days.

18. Remove soap from the mold and place on its side to cut into bars.
19. Allow curing for four to six weeks.

#2 Milk and Clay Soap

Many beauty products are starting to add French Green Clay because of its fine texture and light green color. It is well known as an oil absorber, so it works well in soaps. When adding lye to milk use extra caution since the lye can scorch the milk if too hot and this will leave you with a darker color to your soap as well as an unpleasant smell.

Ingredients:

- [ ] Scalloped Round Mold
- [ ] Impression Mat
- [ ] 4.3 ounces Borage Oil
- [ ] 4.3 ounces Coconut Oil
- [ ] 5.1 ounces Olive Oil
- [ ] 3.4 ounces Palm Oil
- [ ] 2.4 ounces Sodium Hydroxide Lye
- [ ] 5 ounces milk
- [ ] 0.6 ounces Lemongrass Essential Oil
- [ ] 0.4 ounces Tea Tree Essential Oil
- [ ] 2 teaspoons French Green Clay
- [ ] ½ teaspoon Titanium Dioxide

Directions:

1. The first thing you need to do is make sure your milk is properly prepared. When lye is added to milk the temperatures quickly heat to

200 degrees Fahrenheit. This will scorch the milk, causing a dark yellow color and a bad smell. You can help prevent scorching by keeping temperatures as cool as possible. The best option is to freeze the milk into cubes before putting it in the lye.
2. You should also prepare your soap mold by cutting out your desired impression mat design pattern in your desired shape and placing them pattern side up in the round mold.
3. You also want to prepare your coloring. Mix the Titanium Dioxide with ½ tablespoon of lightweight liquid oil. In a second container mix the French Green Clay with 2 tablespoons of distilled water.
4. Slowly add about ¼ of your lye flakes directly to the frozen milk cubes. Then stir together using a non-reactive spoon.
5. After stirring for a few minutes, add another ¼ of your lye flakes and stir for another several minute.
6. Continue this process until you've added all the lye flakes to the milk. The more lye you add, the more the milk will melt.
7. After the milk is completely melted, you should continue to stir until all the lye is dissolved. The cooler temperature of the liquid means the lye will take longer to dissolve.
8. Combine all the oils and completely melt them.
9. Wait for the oils to cool to about 130 degrees Fahrenheit then add in the milk and lye solution.
10. While adding the milk, start using your stick blender. The hard oils may solidify at the cooler temperature of the lye solution, so you want to add gradually in order to prevent a false trace.
11. After you've added all the lye solution, you should continue to blend until you have a thin trace. There may be some graininess, but this is fine.
12. After you achieve a thin trace, you can whisk in the essential oil.
13. Next, add in the French Green Clay. The soap will likely be a thick

texture at this point, but this is fine. Use the stick blender on pulse a few times to get rid of clumps.
14. Add the Titanium Dioxide. If the soap is a thin trace, stick blend; but it if's becoming thick then use a whisk.
15. The soap needs to have a thin texture so you can pour it into the mold cavities and fill in the small details of your impression mat. However, this texture can take a long time to release from a mold. You can stick blend to a medium trace, but you need to be very careful not to over blend.
16. After you have achieved the best texture, slowly pour the soap into the mold. Tap the mold after each cavity is filled in order to get rid of air bubbles.
17. Spritz the top with alcohol in order to prevent soda ash.
18. If your climate is hot, you should place the soap in the refrigerator for several hours to keep the soap cool and prevent the milk from scorching. If your climate is 70 degrees Fahrenheit or less, then you can keep the soap out at room temperature.
19. Let the soap sit for one to two days or until easy to remove from the mold.
20. Allow the soap to sit for one more day then you can remove the impression mat.
21. Allow the soap curing for four to six weeks.

#3 Jade Swirl

Jade is a beautiful green stone that has long been thought to have healing properties. The Jade Fragrance Oil has a very fresh scent of English ivy, jasmine and green apple.

Ingredients:

- ☐ Loaf Mold
- ☐ Hanger Swirl Tool
- ☐ 3.2 ounces Borage Oil
- ☐ 1.2 ounces Castor Oil
- ☐ 10 ounces Coconut Oil
- ☐ 17.6 ounces Olive Oil
- ☐ 8 ounces Palm Oil
- ☐ 5.6 ounces Sodium Hydroxide Lye
- ☐ 11.9 ounces Distilled Water
- ☐ 2 ounces Jade Fragrance Oil
- ☐ 1.5 teaspoons Titanium Dioxide
- ☐ 1 teaspoon Aqua Pearl Mica
- ☐ ½ teaspoon Kelly Green Mica

Directions:

1. Start by preparing your colors. Mix the Aqua Pearl Mica into 1 tablespoon of a lightweight liquid oil of your choice. In a second container mix the Kelly Green Mica with ½ tablespoon of a lightweight liquid oil of your choice.
2. Add lye to the water slowly and carefully, gently stirring until the liquid is clear and the lye is fully dissolved.
3. Melt and combine the oils. Add the Titanium Dioxide and stick blend to remove clumps.
4. After the lye and oils have cooled to 130 degrees Fahrenheit, add them together and stick blend until a thin trace is achieved.
5. Add the Jade Fragrance Oil and whisk until completely mixed.
6. Remove about 500 ml into a smaller container.
7. Add both colors to the larger container of soap. And mix completely

with a whisk.
8. Pour some of the green soap into the mold. Then pour in some of the white soap into the mold from several inches above in order to help the white soap get into the green soap.
9. Continue alternating both soaps until the mold is full. Every time you pour a new batch, tap the mold to get rid of air bubbles. Whisk the soap periodically in order to keep it fluid.
10. Leave a little bit of green and white soap to create a swirl pattern for the top of the soap.
11. Give one last firm tap to get rid of air bubbles.
12. Insert the Hanger Swirl Tool on one side of the mold and make loops in the center of the mold. Continue this motion at different heights inside the mold. The more loops you do, the more swirls you get. How much you do is up to you. Once done a pull-up and out along one side of the mold.
13. Pour the last of the white and green soap along the top in a line pattern you prefer.
14. Spritz the top with alcohol to prevent soda ash.
15. Cover the mold with a lid to insulate the soap. If you live in a warm area, you should check the soap every 30 minutes to make sure it isn't getting too hot and cracking.
16. Allow the soap to sit for two to three days or until you can unmold it easily.
17. Cut the soap into bars and allow to curing for four to six weeks.

#4 Eggnog Soap

Eggnog is a classic holiday drink and popular in the winter months. Eggnog soap comes with a scent of vanilla, nutmeg, caramel, and rum; something that can be enjoyed all year around and not just in the cooler winter months. This soap is similar to milk soaps in the sense that it is a bit more challenging.

Ingredients:

Embeds: ☐ 2 small 9 ball silicone molds
☐ 1-ounce cocoa butter
☐ 2.5 ounces Coconut Oil
☐ 4 ounces Olive Oil
☐ 2.5 ounces Palm Oil
☐ 1.5 ounces Sodium Hydroxide Lye
☐ 3.3 ounces distilled water
☐ 1 tablespoon Cocoa Powder

Base: ☐ Mold with a sliding bottom
☐ Silicone Liner
☐ 4 Egg Yolks
☐ 5.4 ounces Cocoa Butter
☐ 13.5 ounces Coconut Oil
☐ 21.6 ounces Olive Oil
☐ 13.5 ounces Palm Oil
☐ 7.6 ounces Sodium Hydroxide Lye
☐ 17.8 ounces Distilled Water
☐ 3.5 ounces Spiked Eggnog Fragrance Oil
☐ Frosting Bag
☐ 6 teaspoons Titanium Dioxide
☐ ½ teaspoon Yellow Oxide
☐

Directions:

Embeds:

1. Gently stir the lye and water while adding slowly and carefully until fully dissolved and the liquid is clear.
2. Combine and melt the oils. Add the cocoa powder and stir to remove chunks.
3. After everything has cooled to 130 degrees Fahrenheit or less, combine the lye solution and oil solution, blending until you have a very thin trace. Often it is going to require about thirty to sixty seconds of blending and stirring.
4. Once everything is completely mixed, carefully pour into each cavity of the ball molds. After they are full, pour the remaining mixture into a separate mold, it doesn't matter what mold since this soap will be shredded later for the final soap.
5. Let the soap stay in the mold for one to two days or until you can remove it from the mold easily.
6. Use a cheese grater to shred the soap from the extra mold.

Base:
1. Start by preparing your colors. Mix the Titanium Dioxide with 4 tablespoons of a liquid oil of your choice until there are no clumps. In a second container, mix the Yellow Oxide with ½ tablespoon lightweight liquid oil of your choice until there are no clumps.
2. Separate out four egg yolks and whisk together until smooth.
3. Combine the water and lye slowly and carefully. Gently stir until the liquid is clear and the lye is fully dissolved.
4. Melt and combine the oils and then allow them to cool to about 90 degrees Fahrenheit.
5. Add about one ounce of the oils to the egg yolks and whisk quickly. The goal is to slowly raise the temperature of the egg yolks. If the oils are too hot, then you'll end up cooking chunks of egg.
6. Continue adding a small amount of oil and whisking until the egg yolks

achieve a temperature of about 80 degrees Fahrenheit with a smooth and liquid texture.
7. Check the temperature of the lye solution; it should be at 90 degrees Fahrenheit or lower. Slowly pour the lye into the container of oils and start pulsing with a stick blender. Do this for about thirty to sixty second or until you get the consistency of thin pudding.
8. Slowly start adding the egg mixture into the soap batter while pulsing with the stick blender, so the eggs are incorporated quickly. Do this until all the egg mixture is added.
9. Remove 800 ml of the batter into a separate container and add 1 tablespoon of the Titanium Dioxide to it. Whisk until fully mixed and set aside.
10. Add the rest of the Titanium Dioxide to the other soap container and whisk to mix. Then add ¼ teaspoon of Yellow Oxide and whisk until fully mixed.
11. Pour all of the Fragrance Oil into the large soap container and fully mix. Don't add any fragrance to the 800 ml of soap. If the larger soap container is still a very thin texture, you should pulse a few times to thicken.
12. Add all of the shredded soap from the first batch to the large soap container and fully mix.
13. Pour the large container of soap into the mold and spread evenly. Tap the mold on the counter to remove air bubbles.
14. For the white soap, you want a texture that is smooth enough to pipe, but also thick enough to hold shape. Allow it to sit if you need it to harden more. Once it is ready, transfer some to the frosting bag.
15. Start by piping small dollops into the middle of the mold, then on either side to create rows of three.
16. Lastly, place a larger dollop on top of the center dollops to give it height. There is no real specific way; it is simply what looks good to you.

17. Place a soap embed sphere from the earlier stage into the center of each dollop. For the top, you can choose to sprinkle either cinnamon or cappuccino mica based on your skin sensitivity.
18. Spritz the top with alcohol to prevent soda ash.
19. The soap needs to be kept at 70 degrees Fahrenheit or cooler. If you live in a hot area, you can place it in the refrigerator or freezer for five to 24 hours. Keep it in the mold for two days or until it is easy to unmold.
20. Cut into bars and allow to cure for four to six weeks.

#5 Simple Black Tea

Black tea has always been a great way to get antioxidants, and with this recipe, you get those benefits in your soap. The scent is one of the smoky tea leaves and a little amber. This is a wonderful soap that works for everyone and isn't as difficult to make as you may think.

Ingredients:

- ☐ Mold with a sliding bottom
- ☐ Silicone Liner
- ☐ 2.7 ounces Cocoa Butter
- ☐ 13.5 ounces Coconut Oil
- ☐ 2.7 ounces Matcha Green Tea Butter
- ☐ 16.2 ounces Olive Oil
- ☐ 13.5 ounces Palm Oil
- ☐ 5.4 ounces Sweet Almond Oil
- ☐ 14.3 ounces Brewed Black Tea
- ☐ 7.6 ounces Sodium Hydroxide Lye
- ☐ 2 ounces Bergamot Black Tea Fragrance Oil
- ☐ 3 teaspoons Titanium Dioxide

- ☐ 1 teaspoon Activated Charcoal
- ☐ 3 teaspoons Purple Brazilian Clay
- ☐ Black Tea Leaves

Directions:

1. Start by preparing your colors. Add the Titanium Dioxide to 3 tablespoons of a liquid oil of your choice. In a separate container mix the Activated Charcoal with 1 tablespoon of liquid oil. Lastly, use a third container to mix the Purple Brazilian Clay into 3 tablespoons of Distilled Water.
2. Boils 16 ounces of distilled water to prepare your brewed black tea. Allow the tea to be steep and cool for about an hour. Wait for the tea to cool to about 70 degrees Fahrenheit. The cooler the tea, the lighter the color of the lye mixture. You can also freeze the tea and prepare it as you would the milk soap recipe.
3. Add the lye to the black tea slowly and carefully, gently stirring until the lye is fully dissolved. The mixture is likely to have a brown color, and this is fine.
4. Completely mix and melt your oils. After the lye solution and oils have cooled to 130 degrees Fahrenheit or less, then you can combine them and stick blend until you have a thin trace.
5. Once you have a thin trace, you can add the fragrance oil.
6. Remove about 26 ounces of soap into a separate container. To this add 2 teaspoons of the Activated Charcoal and whisk to mix completely.
7. Add all of the Titanium Dioxide into the larger container of soap and fully incorporate with the stick blender. Then split this amount in half, each weighing about 26 ounces.
8. To one half of the Titanium Dioxide mix, you want to add the Purple Brazilian Clay and incorporate with a stick blender.

9. All containers of soap need to be at a medium to thick trace before you start layering.
10. Start by pouring half of the uncolored soap into the mold and spreading evenly, but it doesn't have to be straight.
11. Next, pour half of the black soap onto the white, but don't let the black soap fall through the first white layer. Gently cover it with a spoon and spread evenly.
12. Lastly cover with half of the purple soap, spreading with a spoon. Tap the mold firmly to remove air bubbles.
13. Do this process a second time, using up the rest of the soap.
14. After the final purple layer, use a spoon to create peaks in the center or any other design that looks good to you.
15. Sprinkle the dried black tea leaves on the top of the soap and lightly press in place with gloves.
16. Spritz the top with alcohol to prevent soda ash.
17. Don't cover or insulate this soap; it needs to be kept cool. You can place it in the refrigerator or freezer for several hours if you live in a hot climate. Let is sit in the mold for two to three days or until easily removed.
18. Cut into bars and cure for four to six weeks.

#6 ENERGIZING COFFEE

This is a simple soap recipe for those who love coffee or those who just want a great smelling soap bar.

Ingredients:

- ☐ Loaf Mold
- ☐ 13.9 ounces Olive Oil

- ☐ 8.3 ounces Coconut Oil
- ☐ 8.3 ounces Palm Oil
- ☐ 1.7 ounces Coffee Butter
- ☐ 1 ounce Coffee Oil
- ☐ 5 ounces Brewed Coffee
- ☐ 5 ounces Distilled Water
- ☐ 4.6 ounces Sodium Hydroxide Lye
- ☐ 2 Tablespoons Coffee Grounds
- ☐ Whole Coffee Beans

Directions:

1. Brew your coffee as you want, but the stronger the coffee, the darker your soap will be; just make sure you have five ounces of brewed coffee.
2. Add five ounces of distilled water to the coffee and allow to cool to room temperature before you add the lye.
3. Slowly add the lye to the coffee and gently stir until the lye is completely dissolved. The solution will be dark and smell funny, but this is normal.
4. Combine and melt the oils then allow it to cool to 130 degrees Fahrenheit or less.
5. Once everything has cooled, combine the lye mixture and the oils until a thin trace is achieved.
6. Stick blend the soap until you achieve a medium trace.
7. Add the coffee grounds to the soap and whisk until fully mixed into the soap.
8. Pour the soap into the mold and tap firmly to remove air bubbles.
9. Create the desired texture pattern in the center of the soap.
10. Place coffee beans in the center of the soap the length of the mold and gently press them in with gloved hands.
11. Spritz the top with alcohol to prevent soda ash.

12. Allow the soap to sit in the mold for two to three days or until you can easily remove it from the mold.
13. Cut into bars and allow to cure for four to six weeks.

#7 Simple Orange Zest

Just because you are new to soap making doesn't mean you can't make a unique and interesting soap that looks and smells like you have years of experience. This orange soap recipe is great for beginners because it looks vibrant and smells excellent with only minimal work and can even be done with some soap making kits.

Ingredients:

- ☐ Loaf Mold
- ☐ 33 ounces soap making kit
- ☐ 10 ounces Distilled Water
- ☐ 4.7 ounces Sodium Hydroxide Lye
- ☐ 2 teaspoons Sodium Lactate
- ☐ 1.7 ounces Orange Essential Oil
- ☐ 3 teaspoons Orange Peel Powder
- ☐ Marigold Petals (optional)

Directions:

1. Slowly and carefully mix the lye and water, gently stirring until the lye is completely dissolved and the liquid is clear.
2. Fully melt your soap mix kit until there is no chunks or cloudiness. You can also use your own oil mix if you don't want to use a kit.
3. Once the lye and oils are to a temperature of 130 degrees Fahrenheit or less you can mix them and add in the sodium lactate.

4. Use a stick blender and pulse the mixture. Do this for fifteen to twenty-second and then use the blender to stir the mixture. Continue until the soap is the consistency of thin pudding.
5. Add the Orange Essential Oil to the soap and use the stick blender to completely mix in the fragrance.
6. Add the Orange Peel Powder and blend until there are no clumps and everything is fully incorporated.
7. The soap should have thickened slightly now, and you want to continue to blend until it is the texture of thick pudding and can form peaks.
8. Pour the soap into the loaf mold and tap firmly on the counter to release air bubbles.
9. Using a spoon create a peak down the center of the soap or any other pattern you desire.
10. Sprinkle marigold petals on the top if desired.
11. Spritz the top with alcohol.
12. Allow the soap to harden in the mold for two to three days or until the mold comes away easily.
13. Cut the soap into bars. Then cure the bars an additional four to six weeks.

#8 Amber and Evergreen Soap

The Evergreen tree is known for its fresh and vivid scent as well as its beautiful green color all year long. This soap gives you that same experience in your home with a beautiful scent of pine, cedar, clove, and amber.

Ingredients:

- ☐ Loaf Mold
- ☐ 8.8 ounces Coconut Oil
- ☐ 8.8 ounces Palm Oil

- ☐ 8.8 ounces Olive Oil
- ☐ 3.5 ounces Meadow foam Oil
- ☐ 3.5 ounces Sweet Almond Oil
- ☐ 1.8 ounces Castor Oil
- ☐ 11.5 ounces Distilled Water
- ☐ 4.8 ounces Sodium Hydroxide Lye
- ☐ 2 ounces Cedar and Amber Fragrance Oil
- ☐ ½ teaspoon Yellow Oxide
- ☐ 1 teaspoon Evergreen Mica
- ☐ ½ teaspoon Burgundy Pigment
- ☐ 1 teaspoon Titanium Dioxide

Directions:

1. Prepare your colors. Mix the Titanium Dioxide with 1 tablespoon of a liquid oil of your choice and mix until there are no clumps. In separate containers mix the Yellow Oxide and Burgundy Pigment each with ½ tablespoon of an oil of your choice until there is no clumps. Lastly, mix the Evergreen Mica in 1 tablespoon of oil of your choice until there is no clumps.
2. Mix the water and lye slowly and carefully, gently stirring until the lye is completely dissolved and the liquid is clear.
3. Combine the oils and melt them completely. Once cooled to 130 degrees Fahrenheit or less you can combine them with the lye and stick blend them until you reach a thin trace.
4. Divide the soap into four even containers. Mix each container as follows, whisking to mix the contents fully:
    a. In container, one makes the white color by adding 2 teaspoons Titanium Dioxide.
    b. In container two make the yellow color by adding ¼ teaspoon

       Yellow Oxide.
- c. In container three make the green color by adding all of the Evergreen Mica.
- d. In container four make the red color by adding ¼ teaspoon Burgundy Pigment.
5. Add the fragrance oil evenly to all four containers and whisk to mix completely.
6. If the soap is still at a thin trace, you can use a stick blender and pulse until each container is slightly thick. It is best to have a medium trace soap.
7. Have a large spoon for each color and place one color at a time into the mold in three different spots.
8. Continue plopping spoonful of color into the mold in various areas. You can choose how you want to do this, but make sure you don't layer the same color twice. Occasionally tap the mold firmly to get rid of air bubbles.
9. Use a chopstick or dowel and insert at the top of the soap and then create S-shaped curves down the length of the mold and repeat in the opposite direction.
10. Spritz the top with alcohol to prevent soda ash.
11. Cover the soap to insulate for 24 hours and allow to sit in the mold for two to three days or until easy to remove from the mold.
12. Cut into bars and allow the soap to cure for four to six weeks.

#9 Honey Soap

Honey is a popular additive in many soaps, however making soap with honey is as challenging as use milk and tea. You need to make sure you use the right amount of honey and keep your temperatures cool.

Ingredients:

- ☐ Loaf Mold
- ☐ Bubble wrap to line the mold
- ☐ 1.8 ounces Argan Oil
- ☐ 1.8 ounces Castor Oil
- ☐ 7 ounces Coconut Oil
- ☐ 10.5 ounces Olive Oil
- ☐ 7 ounces Palm Oil
- ☐ 7 ounces Sunflower Oil
- ☐ 4.8 ounces Sodium Hydroxide Lye
- ☐ 11 ounces Distilled Water
- ☐ 2.3 ounces Honey Fragrance Oil
- ☐ 1 tablespoon Honey

Directions:

1. Placing bubble wrap in the bottom of your soap mold will give the final soap a honeycomb appearance. However, you can also use an impression mat if you want to put a specific pattern in your soap or you can have a plain bar of soap; it is up to you.
2. Add lye to the water slowly and carefully, gently stirring until the liquid is clear and the lye is fully dissolved.
3. Combine the oils and melt completely. Once the lye and oils have cooled to around 130 degrees Fahrenheit or lower you can combine them and stick blend until you reach a light trace.
4. Add the honey and stick blend until fully mixed. Alternate between pulses and using the blender to stir.
5. Add the fragrance oil and alternate between pulses and stirring until completely mixed.

6. Continue to mix until you achieve a medium trace.
7. Pour the soap mix into the mold and tap a few times to disperse air bubbles.
8. Even the top with a spatula and immediately place in the refrigerator or freezer for at least three hours and up to 24 hours.
9. Allow the soap to set in the mold for two days or until easy to remove from the mold and peel the bubble wrap.
10. Cut into bars and allow to cure for four to six weeks.

#10 Nettle, Spearmint & Lime

Most people only think of the sting of the nettle weed, but they actually have good therapeutic values that can work well in soap. This soap supplements the value of the nettle weed with the fresh aroma of spearmint and lime.

Ingredients:

- ☐ 20 ounces Vegetable Fat
- ☐ 6 ounces Coconut Oil
- ☐ 6 ounces Palm Oil
- ☐ 12 ounces Distilled Water
- ☐ 4 ¼ ounces Sodium Hydroxide Lye
- ☐ 1 tablespoon Nettle Leaf Powder
- ☐ Dried Nettle Leaf
- ☐ 1 teaspoon Spearmint Essential Oil
- ☐ 2 teaspoons Lime Fragrance Oil

Directions:

1. Add the lye to the water carefully and slowly while gently stirring until the lye is completely dissolved and the liquid is clear.
2. Combine the oils and melt completely. Once everything has cooled to

130 degrees Fahrenheit or less, then you can combine the oils and lye.
3. Once the trace is achieved, remove a small amount of soap mixture and mix in the powdered nettle.
4. Return it to the pan and stir rapidly. Then add the essential oils and mix well.
5. Pour the soap into your desired mold.
6. Allow it to set in the mold for 48 hours or until easy to remove from the mold.
7. Allow it to cure for a couple of weeks then dampen the top of the soap with a little bit of water and rub it into the dried nettle leaf. The cure for another two to three weeks.

MEDICATED SOAP RECIPES

#1 Soothing Aloe Vera Soap

Aloe Vera is great for the skin and has so many health properties I could write an entire book on them. It is safe to say that aloe vera in soap is anti-infective, anti-inflammatory and soothing for burns and cuts. This soap works great for a variety of skin conditions.

Ingredients:

- ☐ 7.5 ounces Distilled Water
- ☐ 3 ounces Sodium Hydroxide Lye
- ☐ 1.5 pounds Olive Oil
- ☐ 0.4 ounces Beeswax
- ☐ 1.8 ounces Aloe Vera Juice
- ☐ 0.18 ounces Mint Essential Oil

Directions:

1. Add the lye to the water carefully and slowly. Gently stir until the lye is completely dissolved and the liquid is clear.
2. Heat the olive oil to 120 to 140 degrees Fahrenheit and then stir in the beeswax slowly.
3. Remove the olive oil from heat and add the lye mixture, stirring slowly.
4. Stir about every 15 minutes until the mixture congeals and thickens.
5. Stir in the Aloe Vera Juice and essential oil. Stir for a minute with a spoon or whisk.
6. Pour the soap into the soap mold of your choice and gently tap to remove

air bubbles.
7. Cover the mold with a towel and allow to sit for two days. Uncover and let stand for another day if the mold is large.
8. Remove from the mold and allow to sit for another day.
9. Cut into bars and allow to cure for one month, occasionally turning for a uniform dry.

#2 Charcoal and Bamboo Soap

Charcoal bamboo powder has a number of skin care benefits but does best for oily skin. The charcoal helps to absorb toxins, impurities, and oils from your skin. It works best for those with acne, psoriasis, and eczema.

Ingredients:

- ☐ 9.6 ounces Palm Oil
- ☐ 8 ounces Olive Oil
- ☐ 8 ounces Coconut Oil
- ☐ 4.8 ounces Palm Kernel Oil
- ☐ 1.6 ounces Castor Oil
- ☐ 1 Tablespoon of Charcoal Bamboo Powder
- ☐ 12.1 ounces Distilled Water
- ☐ 4.7 ounces Sodium Hydroxide Lye

Directions:

1. Add the lye very slowly and carefully to the water and stir gently until fully dissolved and the liquid is clear.
2. Melt a small amount of oils until completely dissolved and mix in the charcoal bamboo powder, then add the rest of the oils and stir until a light trace is achieved.

3. You can add any desired fragrance oil and whisk until fully mixed.
4. Pour into your desired mold and tap to remove air bubbles.
5. Allow to sit about 24 hours or until you can easily remove from the mold.
6. Cut into bars and allows to cure for four to six weeks.

#3 Tea Tree Oil Soap

Tea tree oil is found in a range of natural products because of its many medicinal properties. Tea tree oil is a wonderful antiseptic, antifungal, and antibacterial which makes it great for soap. It is ideal for those with skin conditions such as acne, oily skin, poison ivy, psoriasis and other similar skin conditions.

Ingredients:

- ☐ 7.2 ounces Olive Oil
- ☐ 4.8 ounces Coconut Oil
- ☐ 2.08 ounces Sweet Almond Oil
- ☐ 1.92 ounces Avocado Oil
- ☐ 6.08 ounces Distilled Water
- ☐ 2.27 ounces Sodium Dioxide Lye
- ☐ 0.7 ounces Tea Tree Essential Oil

Directions:

1. Add the lye carefully and slowly to the water. Stir gently until you dissolve all of the lye, and the liquid is clear.
2. Melt the oils together and mix well.
3. Once the oils and lye are around 95 degrees Fahrenheit, slowly combine them and mix with a stick blender until you achieve a light trace.
4. Add the tea tree oil and any fragrance oils you choose and mix until

completely incorporated.
5. Pour the soap into your desired mold and cover for 24 to 48 hours or until easy to remove from the mold.
6. Cut the soap into bars and allow to cure for four to six weeks.

#4 Insecticidal Soap

Summer can be an enjoyable time full of fun, but dealing with insects can quickly spoil the outdoor fun. Citronella and lavender are great for repelling insects so you can enjoy your summer outdoors.

Ingredients:

- ☐ 1 and ½ cups Tallow
- ☐ ½ cup Coconut Oil
- ☐ ¾ cup Distilled Water
- ☐ ¼ cup Sodium Hydroxide Lye
- ☐ 1 teaspoon Citronella Essential Oil
- ☐ 1 teaspoon Eucalyptus Essential Oil
- ☐ 1 teaspoon Lavender Essential Oil

Directions:

1. Melt the Tallow and Coconut oil, setting it aside to cool.
2. Slowly and carefully add lye to the water and gently stir until fully dissolved.
3. Once the oils and lye are 130 degrees Fahrenheit or cooler, then you can combine them while stirring constantly.
4. Stir until the mixture turns creamy and thick.
5. Add the essential oils and whisk to distribute evenly.
6. Pour into your desired molds. Tap to disperse air bubbles.

7. Allow to set 24 to 48 hours or until easy to remove from the mold.
8. Cut into bars and cure for four to six weeks.

#5 LAVENDER AND PEPPERMINT ANTISEPTIC SOAP

When making this antiseptic soap, I prefer to use natural indigo powder to give the soap a beautiful rich blue color. The indigo color also has healing benefits as well. This soap not only has antiseptic properties but can also help with psoriasis, rashes, sores, and eczema.

Ingredients:

- ☐ 16.91 ounces Coconut Oil
- ☐ 13.53 ounces Rice Bran Oil
- ☐ 3.38 ounces Sesame Oil
- ☐ 4.5 ounces Sodium Hydroxide Lye
- ☐ 10.48 ounces Distilled Water
- ☐ ½ ounce Indigo paste or powder
- ☐ ½ ounce Peppermint Essential Oil
- ☐ ½ ounce Lavender Essential Oi

Directions:

1. Add lye to the water slowly and carefully, gently stirring until completely dissolved.
2. Melt the oils and stir until completely combined.
3. Cool oils and lye to about 130 degrees Fahrenheit or less and then combine, stirring until you reach trace.
4. Add the Indigo paste or powder and essential oils, stirring until completely incorporated.
5. Pour into the desired soap mold and tap to remove air bubbles.

6. Allow 24 to 48 hours or until you can easily remove the mold.
7. Cut into bars and allow to cure for four to six weeks.

#6 Soothing Chamomile Soap

Chamomile has long been known for its calming effects. It has been shown to work as an antidepressant, muscle relaxer, and immune system booster. On the outside, chamomile can help with irritated skin, fight acne and lighten your skin. Chamomile soap is very soothing.

Ingredients:

- [ ] 5.6 ounces Olive Oil infused with Chamomile
- [ ] 4.48 ounces Babassu Oil
- [ ] 2.4 ounces Coconut Oil
- [ ] 2.4 ounces Avocado Oil
- [ ] 1.12 ounces Cocoa Butter
- [ ] 2.33 ounces Sodium Hydroxide Lye
- [ ] 6.08 ounces Distilled Water

Directions:

1. Slowly and carefully add lye to the water and gently stir until dissolved.
2. Melt the oils, try to keep the temperature on the low side of under 100 degrees Fahrenheit in order to preserve the properties of the chamomile.
3. Once the oils and lye are cooled, you can combine them and blend until the desired trace is achieved.
4. Add dried chamomile flowers if desired and any essential oils.

5. Pour into the desired mold.
6. Place it in the freezer for a few hours to prevent the gel phase.
7. Allow to sit in the mold for 24 to 48 hours or until easy to remove from the mold.
8. Cut into bars and cure for four to six weeks.

#7 Skin Blemish Soap

Several West African tribes have a traditional, rough soap that has been used for centuries to treat a range of skin conditions. There isn't a set recipe for the soap, as each tribe has variations. But this recipe is developed from all the combinations to develop a soap that works well for skin blemishes such as acne, oily skin, eczema, rashes, and hyperpigmentation.

Ingredients:

- ☐ 8.8 ounces Shea Butter
- ☐ 2.4 ounces Palm Kernel Oil
- ☐ 2.4 ounces Palm Oil
- ☐ 2.4 ounces Coconut Oil
- ☐ 2.21 ounces Sodium Hydroxide Lye
- ☐ 6.08 ounces Distilled Water
- ☐ 1 to 2 teaspoons of African Black Soap Mixture

Directions:

1. Carefully and slowly add the lye to the water and stir until completely dissolved.
2. Melt the Shea Butter and oil, stirring until combined.
3. Allow the oils and lye to cool to 130 degrees Fahrenheit or less then combine, stirring until trace is achieved.

4. Add in the soap mixture until desired texture is achieved.
5. Pour into desired mold and tap to remove air bubbles.
6. Allow to set 24 to 48 hours or until easy to remove from the mold.
7. Cut into bars and allow to cure for four to six weeks.

#8 Acne Fighter

Nothing is more irritating than having acne breakouts and skin blemishes. This recipe is focused on helping your fight your acne.

Ingredients:

- ☐ 14 ounces Tallow
- ☐ 6 ounces Olive Oil
- ☐ 6 ounces Coconut Oil
- ☐ 10 ounces Distilled Water
- ☐ 4 ounces Sodium Hydroxide Lye
- ☐ 0.5 to 1 ounce Tea Tree Oil
- ☐ 1 tablespoon Activated Charcoal Powder

Directions:

1. Slowly and carefully add the lye to the water and gently stir until fully dissolved.
2. Combine and melt the oils, then allow to cool to 100 degrees Fahrenheit.
3. Once the lye is at 100 degrees Fahrenheit or less, you can pour the lye water into the oils.
4. Blend until it thickens like pudding and then add the Tea Tree Oil.
5. Remove one cup of soap mix and whisk in the Activated Charcoal until there are no chunks and then mix back into the main pot of soap.
6. Pour the soap into your desired mold and cover for 24 to 48 hours or

until easy to remove from the mold.
7. Cut into bars and cure for four to six weeks.

#9 Baking Soda and Oatmeal Skin Bar

The ingredients in this soap recipe come together to form the best skin soothing soap bar you'll ever find. This soap is highly nourishing and can also help calm irritated skin. You can either make this bar unscented for sensitive skin, or you can add any preferred mild scent. The oatmeal also provides a gentle exfoliation.

Ingredients:

- ☐ 16 ounces Castile Soap
- ☐ 16 ounces Sodium Bicarbonate
- ☐ 3.2 ounces Distilled Water
- ☐ 0.2 ounces Oat Extract
- ☐ 0.5 ounces Colloidal Oatmeal
- ☐ 0.2 ounces Rolled Oats
- ☐ 0.8 ounces Fragrance or Essential Oil (optional)
- ☐ Loaf Mold with Liner

Directions:

1. I prefer to use Castile Soap as a rebatch for this one. It makes it quick and easy and allows me to make a wonderful soap from batches that didn't turn out as well. However, you can also make this batch from scratch if you choose.
2. Melt the Castile Soap by heating and then set aside.
3. Mix the baking soda with the Distilled Water and whisk to combine.
4. Add the baking soda water to the melted soap and stir.
5. Add in the Colloidal Oatmeal when the rebatch is starting to become a

paste.
6. Add in the Oat Extract and continue to stir.
7. Wait about twenty minutes until the rebatch starts to thicken into an oatmeal-like texture. If you notice any cracking or clay-like consistency you may need to add a little extra Distilled Water.
8. The mixture is ideal when it reaches the texture of mashed potatoes.
9. Gently pour the soap base into the mold and tap to remove air bubbles. Sprinkle rolled oats on the top.
10. Sit two to four days or until easy to remove from the mold.
11. Cut into bars, and it is ready to go, no need to cure.

#10 Yogurt Soap

There are plenty of healthy reasons to add yogurt to your soap. Yogurt not only contains zinc and lactic acid, but it also has antibacterial properties. This soap can help dry out acne while promoting skin health. The lactic acid will help exfoliate and cleanse your skin. Lastly, it is very moisturizing for your skin.

Ingredients:

- ☐ 3.2 ounces Coconut Oil
- ☐ 1.6 ounces Kokum Butter
- ☐ 11.2 ounces Pomace Olive Oil
- ☐ 5.35 ounces Organic Plain Yogurt
- ☐ 2.15 ounces Sodium Hydroxide Lye
- ☐ ½ teaspoon Sea Salt

Directions:

1. Make sure the yogurt is cold and refrigerated before you start, you may even want to freeze it briefly. Just as you did with the milk recipe.

2. Pour the lye into the yogurt and mix until all the lye is dissolved. The yogurt will turn a bright yellow, and some clumps may develop, this is normal; along with the chemical smell.
3. Combine the oils and butter and melt together.
4. Once both mixtures are cooled to about 95 degrees Fahrenheit, you can mix the Sea Salt into the lye mix.
5. Pour the lye mixture into the oils and butter. Mix until you achieve trace. The consistency is that of pudding.
6. Pour the soap into your desired mold. Cover with a plastic wrap or parchment paper.
7. Let set for 24 hours and then remove from the mold.
8. Cut into bars and cure for one to two months.

HOT PROCESS SOAP RECIPES

FLORAL SCENTED SOAP RECIPES

#1 Frankincense Soap

This refreshing soap will help wake you up in the morning. This is a great soap to get you started when making hot process soaps.

Ingredients:

- ☐ 15 ounces Coconut Oil
- ☐ 15 ounces Olive Oil
- ☐ 12 ounces Sweet Almond Oil
- ☐ 6 ounces Shea Butter
- ☐ 1.5 ounces Castor Oil
- ☐ 15 ounces Distilled Water
- ☐ 7.2 ounces Sodium Hydroxide Lye
- ☐ 1 to 2 tablespoons of Nettle Powder
- ☐ 1-ounce Spearmint Essential Oil
- ☐ 1-ounce Frankincense Essential Oil
- ☐ 0.5-ounce Eucalyptus Essential Oil

Directions:

1. Melt the oils on low in a crockpot. Once they are completely melted, add in the Nettle Powder.
2. In a separate bowl add your lye to the water. Gently stir until the lye is dissolved and set aside to cool.
3. Mix together your essential oils.
4. Once the oils have completely melted, carefully pour in the lye solution.

Blend for about five minutes or until you achieve trace, the texture of stiff pudding.
5. Cook the mixture, if it climbs the walls of the crockpot stir it back down.
6. The mixture is ready when it becomes translucent. You should also be able to roll up a small ball and have it feel waxy.
7. Turn the crockpot off and allow it to cool for a few minutes. Add the essential oils and stir them in completely.
8. Spoon your soap into the mold of your choice and set aside to cool for a few hours or overnight.
9. Remove your soap from the mold and enjoy.

#2 Rosemary Mint Soap

Rosemary and mint is a wonderful combination to have soap. The fresh mint scent is refreshing while the rosemary helps provide a calm element.

Ingredients:

- ☐ 10 ounces Olive Oil
- ☐ 8 ounces Coconut Oil
- ☐ 4 ounces Sunflower Oil
- ☐ 4 ounces Castor Oil
- ☐ 2 ounces Jojoba Oil
- ☐ 3.82 ounces Sodium Hydroxide Lye
- ☐ 10 ounces Distilled Water
- ☐ 1 tablespoon Peppermint
- ☐ 1 teaspoon Rosemary

Directions:

1. Carefully add lye to the water and mix until fully dissolved and cool for fifteen to twenty minutes.

2. Combine the oils and melt in a crock pot until the temperature is between 90 and 100 degrees Fahrenheit.
3. Carefully pour lye into the oils and stir along with stick blending the mix until trace is achieved.
4. Set the slow cooker to low and cook for one hour, stirring every fifteen minutes.
5. Stir in the essential oils, then spoon into your desired mold.
6. Allow the soap to rest for 24 hours before cutting the soap, and it is ready to use.

#3 Calendula Summer Soap

The calendula flower is a summer scent that blends well with the other ingredients in this soap. This is a great soap for a year-round enjoyable summer scent.

Ingredients:

- ☐ 10 ounces Distilled Water
- ☐ 3.9 ounces Sodium Hydroxide Lye
- ☐ 7.5 ounces Coconut Oil
- ☐ 3.5 ounces Cocoa Butter
- ☐ 12.5 ounces Olive Oil infused with Calendula
- ☐ 3.5 ounces Sunflower Oil
- ☐ 1 ounce Castor Oil
- ☐ 1 ounce Tangerine Essential Oil
- ☐ 1 ounce Orange Essential Oil
- ☐ 1 tablespoon finely powdered Oatmeal

Directions:

1. Set your crockpot to low and put your measured oils into the crock pot until melted completely.
2. While the oils are melting, mix your lye and water.
3. Pour your lye mix into the crock pot after a little cooldown period.
4. Blend the mix until trace is achieved, the mix will look like pudding.
5. Put the lid on your crockpot and keep an eye on it as it goes through the stages. If the soap moves up the side, stir it down.
6. Once the soap reaches a mashed potatoes consistency cook for about another fifteen minutes.
7. Turn off the crockpot and allow the mix to sit for five to ten minutes. Then add your essential oils and oatmeal. Stirring well to mix entirely.
8. Pour the soap into your desired mold.
9. Allow the soap to cool completely then remove from the mold, and you're good to go.

#4 Lavender Soap

This is a simple white soap with lavender buds and fragrance oil, so it is a good recipe to start with if you are new to soap making.

Ingredients:

- ☐ 12 ounces Sweet Almond Oil
- ☐ 12 ounces Coconut Oil
- ☐ 3 ounces Shea Butter
- ☐ 4 ounces Sodium Hydroxide Lye
- ☐ 9 ounces Distilled Water
- ☐ 2 tablespoons Dried Lavender Buds
- ☐ 50 drops Lavender Essential Oil

Directions:

1. Add the oils and butter to the crockpot and start warming on low.
2. In a second container, carefully add the lye to the water and stir until dissolved.
3. Wait for the lye temperature drop to around 130 degrees Fahrenheit.
4. Carefully pour the lye into the crockpot of melted oils.
5. Carefully blend the mix until trace is achieved.
6. Cover the crockpot and cook on low heat for about 3 hours, stirring about every 30 minutes or when it starts to climb the sides.
7. Add your essential oils once the soap is ready and the lavender buds, stirring well.
8. Pour the soap mixture into your desired mold and wait until firm.
9. Remove from the mold, and it is ready to use.

#5 Honey and Chamomile Soap

This recipe combines the calming scent of chamomile along with the nourishing effects of honey.

Ingredients:

- 10 ounces Olive Oil
- 8 ounces Coconut Oil
- 4 ounces Castor Oil
- 2 ounces Avocado Oil
- 2 ounces Shea Butter
- 2 ounces Sweet Almond Oil
- 10 ounces Chamomile Tea cooled
- 3.93 ounces Sodium Hydroxide Lye
- 1 tablespoon Honey mixed in 1 tablespoon Distilled Water

Directions:

1. To make the Chamomile Tea, you should boil about 10 ounces of Distilled Water and pour over a cup of fresh Chamomile flowers. Or you can simply buy Chamomile Tea from the store.
2. Make your lye solution by adding your lye to the water and stirring until fully dissolved. Set aside to cool for about ten minutes while preparing your oils.
3. Turn your crockpot on low and add the oils and butter to melt, when the temperature reaches 90 to 100 degrees Fahrenheit.
4. Pour the lye solution into the oils and stir for about 30 seconds.
5. Blend for another minute or so until trace is reached.
6. Make sure your crockpot is on low and cook the mixture for an hour, check every fifteen minutes and stirring if it starts moving up the sides.
7. Once the mixture is done the cooking, let it sit for a few minutes before stirring in the honey/water mixture along with essential oils.
8. Spoon the soap into your desired mold.
9. Let the soap sit overnight to harden.
10. Remove from the mold and cut if desired and you're ready to go.

#6 BEAUTIFUL ROSE SOAP

This beautiful soap makes a wonderful gift or a beautifully scented soap to use yourself.

Ingredients:

- ☐ 8 ounces Olive Oil
- ☐ 6 ounces Coconut Oil
- ☐ 4 ounces Shea Butter

- ☐ 4 ounces Sweet Almond Oil
- ☐ 4 ounces Cocoa Butter
- ☐ 0.75 ounce Castor Oil
- ☐ 10.17 ounces Distilled Water
- ☐ 3.7 ounces Sodium Hydroxide Lye
- ☐ 1 ½ to 2 tablespoons Madder Root Powder
- ☐ Rose Petals
- ☐ 1.25 ounces Palmarosa Essential Oil
- ☐ 0.75-ounce Frankincense Essential Oil
- ☐ 0.25 to 0.50 ounce Benzoin Essential Oil

Directions:

1. Melt the oils in a crockpot on low heat.
2. Add your lye to the water in a separate container and stir until fully dissolved.
3. Carefully pour the lye into the oils and mix until trace is achieved.
4. Cook the mixture, stirring occasionally and when it starts climbing the walls.
5. Once the mixture is cooked to translucency, turn off the heat and allow to cool for a few minutes.
6. Add in the Madder Root Powder and essential oils. Stir until completely blended.
7. Spoon the soap into your desired mold.
8. Sprinkle the Rose Petals on the top and lightly press them into the soap.
9. Allow to cool overnight.
10. Remove from the mold and cut into the desired shape.

#7 LILAC SWIRL

This is a simple and basic recipe. It has a beautiful, elegant scent with vibrant color.

Ingredients:

- 8.8 ounces Rapeseed Oil
- 8.8 ounces Sunflower Oil
- 5.2 ounces Camelina Seed Oil
- 3.5 ounces Soybean Oil
- 3.5 ounces Coconut Oil
- 1.7 ounces Babassu Oil
- 1.7 ounces Castor Oil
- 1.7 ounces Shea Butter
- 1.7 ounces Macadamia Nut Oil
- 0.1 ounce Violet
- 0.8-ounce Lilac Fragrance Oil
- 13 ounces Distilled Water
- 4.8 ounces Sodium Dioxide Lye

Directions:

1. Carefully add your lye to the water until fully dissolved.
2. Melt your oils and butter together in a crockpot on low.
3. Add the lye to the oils once cooled slightly and blend until trace is achieved.
4. Cook the soap for about two hours and occasionally stir or as the soap climbs up the sides.
5. Once the soap has cooled to about 50 degrees Fahrenheit, you can add in the fragrance and coloring and blend only slightly.
6. Pour the soap into your desired mold.
7. Allow to harden overnight then remove from the mold, and you are

ready to go.

#8 Dandelion Soap

Dandelions are a bright and cheerful flower, just like this soap made with their scent. It is a cheerful looking and delightfully scented soap for use year round.

Ingredients:

- ☐ 11 ounces Olive Oil infused with Dandelion
- ☐ 7 ounces Coconut Oil
- ☐ 4 ounces Castor Oil
- ☐ 3 ounces Sweet Almond Oil
- ☐ 3 ounces Cocoa Butter
- ☐ 10 ounces Distilled Water
- ☐ 3.9 ounces Sodium Hydroxide Lye
- ☐ 0.88 ounce Orange Essential Oil
- ☐ 0.35-ounce Grapefruit Essential Oil
- ☐ 0.18-ounce Lemongrass Essential Oil
- ☐ 1 teaspoon Honey mixed with 1 teaspoon Distilled Water

Directions:

1. Start by mixing your lye into the water and stirring until fully dissolved.
2. Turn your crockpot on to low heat and place the oils and butter in to melt, bringing the temperature up to about 90 to 100 degrees Fahrenheit.
3. Pour the lye solution into the oils and stir for 30 seconds. Then blend for

a minute or two. Continue to alternate this way until you reach trace.
4. Make sure your crockpot is on low and cover the soap to cook for about an hour while stirring if needed every fifteen minutes.
5. Once the soap is done the cooking, allow it to cool for a few minutes before stirring in the essential oils and honey mixture.
6. Spoon to the soap into your desired mold.
7. Allow the soap to sit overnight and harden.
8. Remove from the mold and slice into desired bars.

#9 LAVENDER ROSEMARY SOAP

This is a wonderfully elegant soap. The lavender and rosemary are two very calming scents and then adding vanilla make it a very mild soap. This is complemented by the pink clay and lavender flowers.

Ingredients:

- ☐ 15 ounces Coconut Oil
- ☐ 15 ounces Olive Oil
- ☐ 12 ounces Sweet Almond Oil
- ☐ 6 ounces Shea Butter
- ☐ 1.5 ounces Castor Oil
- ☐ 15 ounces Distilled Water
- ☐ 7.2 ounces Sodium Hydroxide Lye
- ☐ 1 ounce Lavender Essential Oil
- ☐ 0.5 ounce Rosemary Essential Oil
- ☐ 1.5 ounces Vanilla Extract
- ☐ 3 tablespoons French Pink Clay
- ☐ 3 tablespoons Lavender Flowers

Directions:

1. Turn your crockpot on low and add the oils and butter together so they can melt completely. You can also add the clay at this time.
2. While the oils are melting prepare your lye solution. Carefully add lye to the water and stir gently until fully dissolved.
3. Once the oils are completely melted, gently pour the lye into the crock pot.
4. Mix the soap until your achieve trace or the point when the soap is like stiff pudding.
5. Cover your crock pot and allow the soap to cook and stir regularly. Once the soap is completely translucent, you are ready to go.
6. Pour the soap into your desired mold.
7. Allow the mixture to cool until hard.
8. Remove from the mold and cut into the desired shape.

#10 Eucalyptus and Lavender Soap

This is a rustic looking soap with a strong outdoor scent. The Eucalyptus and Lavender balance each other nicely for a wonderful scent.

Ingredients:

- ☐ 35 ounces Soybean Oil
- ☐ 176 ounces Olive Oil
- ☐ 17 ounces Coconut Oil
- ☐ 9.7 ounces Sodium Hydroxide Lye
- ☐ 23 ounces Distilled Water
- ☐ Eucalyptus Oil
- ☐ Lavender Flower Buds

Directions:

1. Turn the crockpot on low heat and place your oils into it.
2. Carefully add your lye to the water and gently stir until fully dissolved.
3. Pour lye solution into your oils and gently stir, it will come to trace quickly.
4. Blend on low speed until you achieve medium trace.
5. Let the soap cook and stir about every 20 minutes, until the soap is translucent.
6. Pour in the Eucalyptus oil and stir completely.
7. Add in the lavender flower buds and stir well.
8. Pour into your desired mold.
9. Allow hardening for 24 hours then remove from mold and cut into desired bars.

UNIQUE SOAPS

#1 Icy Blue Soap

The focus of this soap is to provide an icy blue color and a refreshing scent. In the end, you get a beautiful blue and sparkling soap bar with a refreshing mint scent.

Ingredients:

- ☐ Loaf Mold
- ☐ Silicone Liner
- ☐ 22 ounces Soap Quick Mix
- ☐ 3.1 ounces Sodium Hydroxide Lye
- ☐ 7.3 ounces Distilled Water
- ☐ 0.7-ounce Sodium Lactate
- ☐ 1-ounce Snowdrop Fragrance Oil
- ☐ 0.2-ounce Peppermint Essential Oil
- ☐ ½ teaspoon Caribbean Blue Mica
- ☐ Snowflake Sparkle Mica

Directions:

1. Start by preparing your coloring; mix the Caribbean Blue Mica in ½ tablespoon of a liquid oil of your choice.
2. Start by preparing your lye. Carefully add the lye to the water and gently stir until the lye is completely dissolved.
3. Allow the lye solution to cool to about 130 degrees Fahrenheit then add the sodium lactate.

4. Completely melt the bag of Quick Mix until clear and then place 22 ounces into your crock pot on low.
5. Slowly add the lye solution into the oils, make sure you don't fill the crock pot over half full.
6. Use a stick blender to mix until trace is achieved.
7. Place the lid on the crockpot and cook for about ten minutes. If the middle of the soap isn't changing, you'll want to stir to ensure even cooking.
8. Watch the soap closely in the first 30 minutes. If it is expanding too much up to the sides, then remove from heat and stir it back down.
9. Once the soap is the consistency of thin mashed potatoes, it is likely ready.
10. Add 1 teaspoon of the Caribbean Blue Mica and thoroughly mix.
11. Add a ½ tablespoon of Snowflake Sparkle Mica and mix thoroughly.
12. Slowly add the fragrance and essential oils and stir in well.
13. Spoon the soap into your mold and tap to help it settle then smooth the top.
14. Sprinkle the top with Snowflake Sparkle Mica and gently press into the top with gloved hands.
15. Allow the soap to harden for one to two days. Remove from the mold and cut into bars.

#2 Irish Rain

This soap seems like a simple layer bar with gold accents, but making layered soap with the hot process method can be a bit challenging. However, it is worth the effort for this beautiful looking and refreshing scented soap bar.

Ingredients:

- ☐ Loaf Mold
- ☐ 10.2 ounces Coconut Oil
- ☐ 10.2 ounces Olive Oil
- ☐ 8.5 ounces Rice Bran Oil
- ☐ 3.4 ounces Shea Butter
- ☐ 1.7 ounces Avocado Oil
- ☐ 1-ounce Sodium Lactate
- ☐ 4.7 ounces Sodium Hydroxide Lye
- ☐ 11.2 ounces Distilled Water
- ☐ 2.5 Rain Fragrance Oil
- ☐ 1 teaspoon Chrome Green Oxide
- ☐ Gold Sparkle Mica

Directions:

1. Start by preparing your coloring. Mix the Chrome Green Oxide into 1 tablespoon of a liquid oil of your choice.
2. Next prepare your lye solution by slowly and carefully adding the lye to the water and gently stirring until completely dissolved.
3. Allow the lye solution to cool to about 130 degrees Fahrenheit and then add the sodium lactate.
4. Melt and combine the oils and butter then pour into your crockpot on low heat. Slowly add the lye water.
5. Use a stick blender to mix until you achieve a thick trace.
6. Put the lid on the crockpot and cook for fifteen minutes before checking.
7. For the first 30 minutes, keep a close eye on the soap and remove from heat and stir down any time it starts to get too high.
8. The soap is ready when it looks like glossy mashed potatoes.
9. Add the fragrance oil and mix well, turn off the crockpot.
10. Remove about 300 ml of soap into a container and add 2 teaspoons of

the Chrome Green Oxide and mix the color thoroughly. Place this soap in the bottom of the mold and tap to evenly distribute. Sprinkle the Sparkle Gold Mica evenly across the top, but keep the layer thin.

11. Remove another 300 ml of soap into a different container and add ½ teaspoon of the Chrome Green Oxide and mix the color thoroughly. Pour this soap on top of the first layer and spread gently with a spoon or spatula. Tap the mold to help evenly spread the soap. Sprinkle another thin layer of Sparkle Gold Mica evenly across the top.
12. Scoop out another 300 ml of soap into a third container and add ¼ teaspoon of the Chrome Green Oxide and stir thoroughly. Layer this soap on top of the first two layers in the same manner as the last layer and again place a thin layer of Sparkle Gold Mica on top.
13. Scoop out the remaining soap and add a ⅛ teaspoon of the Chrome Green Oxide and stir thoroughly. Place this soap on top of the last three layers in the same way that you've been doing. And place a thin layer of Sparkle Gold Mica on top.
14. Allow the soap to harden for one to two days.
15. Remove from mold and cut into bars.

#3 FRUIT CLAY BAR

This soap has a natural, marbled effects with the flair of Calendula petals and a lovely mix of fruit scents.

Ingredients:

- 1.2 ounces Avocado Butter
- 2.3 ounces Avocado Oil
- 5.8 ounces Coconut Oil
- 6.9 ounces Olive Oil

- ☐ 5.8 ounces Palm Oil
- ☐ 1.2 ounces Shea Butter
- ☐ 3.3 ounces Sodium Hydroxide Lye
- ☐ 7.7 ounces Distilled Water
- ☐ 0.7-ounce Sodium Lactate
- ☐ 0.5 ounce Fresh Mango Fragrance Oil
- ☐ 0.5-ounce Kumquat Fragrance Oil
- ☐ 1 teaspoon Dark Red Brazilian Clay
- ☐ 1 teaspoon Yellow Silt Clay
- ☐ Calendula Petals

Directions:

1. Prepare your colors. Mix each color in its own container with 1 tablespoon of distilled water until there are no clumps.
2. Prepare your lye solution by mixing the lye into the water slowly and carefully until fully dissolved. Allow to cool to at least 130 degrees Fahrenheit before adding the sodium lactate.
3. Melt and combine the oils and butter. Pour the oils into the crockpot on low heat and then slowly add the lye.
4. Stick blend the soap until a thick trace is achieved.
5. Put the lid on the crockpot and cook for 15 minutes before checking. Don't leave the soap unattended for the first 30 minutes of cooking and remove from heat to stir in the soap starts climbing up the sides of the crockpot.
6. The soap is ready when it achieves the texture of mashed potatoes.
7. Add the fragrance oils and mix well.
8. Split the soap into three even parts, leaving one in the crock pot and moving the other two to separate containers to add the clays.
    a. Color one container with all of the yellow silt clay.
    b. Color the second container with all of the red Brazilian clay.

9. Stir all colors until well blended.
10. Move all of the uncolored soap left in the crock pot to one side. Spoon the red colored soap next to the uncolored soap, leaving room for the yellow colored soap beside the red soap.
11. Use a wooden dowel or chopstick and swirl the three colors together by moving the tool from one side of the crockpot to the other, do so several times until slightly combined.
12. Spoon the soap into the mold and tap on the counter between each scoop.
13. After you've transferred all the soap, top with the Calendula petals and press gently into the soap with gloves.

#4 Spiced Apple Soap

Nothing is better than the smell of apples and spice. It is wonderful on a cold winter day or any time you want to take a relaxing bath or shower.

Ingredients:

- ☐ 18 ounces Canola Oil
- ☐ 8 ounces Coconut Oil
- ☐ 18 ounces Olive Oil
- ☐ 12 ounces Distilled Water
- ☐ 6 ounces Sodium Hydroxide Lye
- ☐ 1 tablespoon Apple Pie Spice
- ☐ 1 tablespoon Turmeric
- ☐ 2 tablespoons Apple Fragrance Oil

Directions:

1. Preheat the oven to 200 degrees Fahrenheit.

2. In a separate container, add the lye to the water slowly and carefully. Allow to cool to 100 degrees Fahrenheit after fully dissolved.
3. Melt your oils together and allow to cool to 100 degrees Fahrenheit.
4. Mix the lye solution into the oils and stick blend until a light trace is achieved.
5. Add spices and then add the fragrance oil.
6. Cover with a lid and put it in the oven for 1 and ½ hours.
7. Scoop the soap into your desired mold.
8. Allow hardening for 24 hours then remove from the mold and cut into bars.

#5 Vanilla Latte Soap

Nothing is better than the scent of coffee and mirroring it with the calming scent of vanilla. This is a great soap to get you started in the morning or to relax after a long, hard day.

Ingredients:

- ☐ 12 ounces Cold Coffee
- ☐ 18 ounces Olive Oil
- ☐ 6 ounces Palm Oil
- ☐ 8 ounces Coconut Oil
- ☐ 2 tablespoons Ground Coffee
- ☐ 2 tablespoons Vanilla Essential Oil
- ☐ 4.8 ounces Sodium Hydroxide Lye

Directions:

1. Prepare the lye by slowly adding it to the coffee. Stir the lye until fully dissolved.

2. Add the oils to your crock pot and turn on high to melt.
3. Pour the lye mixture into the oils once they are completely melted and stir with a wooden spoon to incorporate.
4. Stir constantly for fifteen to thirty minutes until a thick set pudding trace is achieved.
5. Put the lid on the crockpot and allow the soap to cook for ten minutes.
6. Stir the soap the replace the lid to cook for another five to ten minutes.
7. Continue to stir until the mix looks like mashed potatoes.
8. Add the almond oil and ground coffee, mixing well but leaving a slightly swirled appearance.
9. Place the soap in your desired mold and allow to cool.
10. Cut soap into desired bars.

#5 Warm Cider Soap

Apples, cinnamon, clove, and allspice have a warming aroma and calming scent. Not only does this soap smell great when making it, but it is also a wonderfully rich moisturizing soap.

Ingredients:

- 3.5 ounces Sodium Hydroxide Lye
- 9 ounces Distilled Water
- 15 ounces Palm Oil
- 5 ounces Coconut Oil
- 2 ounces Rice Bran Oil
- 2 ounces Shea Butter
- 1 ounce Castor Oil
- 1-ounce Warm Cider Fragrance Oil

Directions:

1. Carefully add lye to the water in a separate bowl and gently stir until completely dissolved.
2. Place your oils and butter in a crockpot on low heat to melt.
3. Once the oils and butter are melted, pour the lye mixture into the crockpot and stir gently.
4. Using a stick blender, blend for two to three minutes until you have a thick, pudding-like consistency.
5. Cover the crockpot and allow the soap base to cook for about an hour or until it looks like mashed potatoes.
6. Turn the crockpot off and add the fragrance oil and stir until well combined.
7. Scoop your soap into your desired mold.
8. Gently tap the mold a few times to remove any air pockets.
9. Allow the soap to harden for 48 hours.
10. Remove from the mold and cut into bars.

#7 Orange Spice Soap

To me, nothing smells better than the combination of vibrant orange and warm cinnamon. Give this unique blend a try with this soap recipe.

Ingredients:

- ☐ Loaf Mold
- ☐ Silicone Liner
- ☐ 22 ounces Quick Mix
- ☐ 3.2 ounces Sodium Hydroxide Lye
- ☐ 7.3 ounces Distilled Water
- ☐ 0.7-ounce Sodium Lactate

- ☐ 0.7 ounce Orange Essential Oil
- ☐ 0.3 ounce Cinnamon Essential Oil
- ☐ 1 tablespoon Orange Peel Powder
- ☐ Anise Stars
- ☐ Dried Orange Slices

Directions:

1. Add lye to the water slowly and carefully, gently stirring until completely dissolved. Cool to 130 degrees Fahrenheit and then add the sodium lactate.
2. Completely melt the quick mix until it is clear. Measure 22 ounces into your crock pot.
3. Slowly add the lye to the oils, don't fill beyond halfway on your crock pot.
4. Stick blend until a thick trace is achieved.
5. Replace the lid on the crockpot and cook for about 10 minutes before checking progress. Remove from heat and stir in the soap expands too far up the sides of the crockpot.
6. Stir the soap regularly for even cooking and allow to cook until the texture of mashed potatoes.
7. Add the Orange Peel Powder and stir to remove any clumps.
8. Add the essential oil and blend until completely incorporated.
9. Spoon the soap into your mold and tap firmly to help it settle. Smooth the top with a spoon or gloved hand.
10. Place the dried orange slices on the top of the soap with an anise star in front.
11. Allow the soap to harden for at least 24 hours then remove and cut into bars.

#8 Honey Vanilla Soap

This is a simple soap bar that is very soothing with a warm and calming fragrance.

Ingredients:

- ☐ 8 ounces Coconut Oil
- ☐ 10 ounces Olive Oil
- ☐ 6 ounces Tallow
- ☐ 3 ounces Shea Butter
- ☐ 4 ounces Castor Oil
- ☐ 10 ounces Distilled Water
- ☐ 4.37 ounces Sodium Hydroxide Lye
- ☐ 2 ounces Beeswax
- ☐ 1 ounce Jojoba Oil
- ☐ 2 tablespoons Honey Powder reconstituted with a ½ tablespoon water
- ☐ 30 ml Vanilla Fragrance Oil

Directions:

1. Carefully add lye to the water and stir until completely dissolved. Allow the mixture to cool.
2. Combines your oils, butter, tallow, and beeswax into a crock pot to melt on low heat.
3. Once melted, pour the lye mixture into the oils and stir.
4. Stir with a stick blender for about two to three minutes until it is a thick pudding-like consistency.
5. Cover the crockpot with lid and allow the soap to cook for about an

hour, occasionally checking to make sure it is cooking evenly. If it is climbing the sides of the crockpot, then remove from heat and stir.
6. Once it is the consistency of mashed potatoes, you should remove the crock pot from the base and add the honey powder, jojoba oil, and fragrance oil. Stir until well combined.
7. Scoop the soap into your mold and gently tap to remove air pockets.
8. Allow the soap to harden for 48 hours then remove from the mold and cut into bars.

#9 Cranberry Soap

Cranberries bring to mind a bright and spicy feeling and this soap replicates that vibrant red color as well as scents that bring out the familiar smell of cranberry sauce. Since you can make this soap in a variety of batch sizes I've based the ingredients on percentages.

Ingredients:

- ☐ 25% Olive Oil
- ☐ 25% Coconut Oil
- ☐ 30% Tallow
- ☐ 15% Shea Butter
- ☐ 5% Castor Oil

Per 1.1 pounds of oils add the following:
- ☐ 1 tablespoon Kaolin Clay
- ☐ 1 teaspoon Titanium Dioxide
- ☐ ½ teaspoon Red Iron Oxide
- ☐ 1 ½ teaspoon Australian Pink Clay
- ☐ 15 grams Orange Essential Oil
- ☐ 15 grams Cinnamon Essential Oil

Directions:

1. Follow the standard soap making instructions until you achieve medium trace.
2. Add the clay, titanium dioxide, red iron oxide, Australian clay and essential oils and return to a medium trace.
3. Scoop the soap into your desired mold and tap on the counter to remove air bubbles.
4. Allow the soap to harden for at least 24 hours and then remove the mold and cut into bars.

#10 PINE AND PEPPERMINT

This is a very refreshing shampoo with a striking green color. It makes an excellent gift for anyone.

Ingredients:

- 8 ounces Olive Oil
- 6 ounces Coconut Oil
- 4 ounces Sweet Almond Oil
- 4 ounces Shea Butter
- 4 ounces Cocoa Butter
- 0.75 ounce Castor Oil
- 10.17 ounces Distilled Water
- 3.7 ounces Sodium Hydroxide Lye
- 2 tablespoons Spirulina Powder
- 1.25 ounces Pine Essential Oil
- 0.75 ounces Peppermint Essential Oil

Directions:

1. Put your oils in a crockpot on low to start melting.

2. Carefully add the lye to the water and gently stir until completely dissolved.
3. Carefully pour the lye into the melted oils in the crock pot.
4. Blend the soap until trace is achieved.
5. Replace the lid on the crockpot and cook the soap.
6. Once the soap is the consistency of mashed potatoes, you can turn off the crockpot and allow the soap to cool for five minutes.
7. Add the coloring and essential oils. Stir in well and mix thoroughly.
8. Scoop your soap into your desired mold.
9. Allow the soap to cool overnight and then remove from the mold and cut into bars.

MEDICATED SOAP RECIPES

#1 Skin Lotion Bar

If you've ever suffered from a skin condition, you know how irritating it can be. You've likely tried a number of skin creams and not found adequate relief. The following is a wonderful rich recipe that creates a lotion bar to help keep your skin moisturized and reduce irritation from a number of common skin conditions such as psoriasis.

Ingredients:

- ☐ Equal parts Beeswax
- ☐ Equal parts Shea Butter
- ☐ Equal parts Coconut Oil
- ☐ 2 tablespoons Vitamin E Oil

Directions:

1. Turn the crockpot on high and allow everything to melt for about an hour, checking occasionally.
2. While waiting for your ingredients to melt, prepare the desired mold. I often find a muffin pan with muffin papers is a good option since it creates nice sized bars.
3. Once the mix is melted, use a ladle to fill the cups ½ full. The mix should give you about 48 bars.
4. Place the pans in the refrigerator for about 10 to 20 minutes or until solid.
5. Remove from the pan, and you are ready to go.

#2 Avocado Hair Rescue Bars

When you make shampoo bars, you don't often think of them as being used for hair. However, I've discovered these wonderful avocado bars do wonders for your hair. Using these leaves your hair shiny and soft, but can also be used for your body and hands as well.

Ingredients:

- ☐ 10 ounces Distilled Water
- ☐ 4.25 ounces Sodium Hydroxide Lye
- ☐ 8 ounces Coconut Oil
- ☐ 3 ounces Avocado Butter
- ☐ 3 ounces Shea Butter
- ☐ 4 ounces Castor Oil
- ☐ 8 ounces Olive Oil
- ☐ 5 ounces Rice Bran Oil
- ☐ 2 tablespoons Lemongrass Essential Oil

Directions:

1. Carefully add the lye to the water and gently stir until completely dissolved. Set aside and allow to cool for about ten minutes.
2. Melt the Coconut Oil, Shea Butter and Avocado Butter over low heat. Place the other liquid oils in the crock pot. Pour the melted butter and coconut oil into the other oils to bring the temperature up to about 90 to 100 degrees Fahrenheit.
3. Pour lye solution into the oils and stir the solution for 30 seconds. Then blend for a minute or two. Alternate between the two until you achieve trace.

4. Turn your crockpot on low and cook the soap for one hour, checking every 15 minutes and stirring if needed.
5. Once the soap is the consistency of mashed potatoes, it is done, and you can then stir in any extra you want.
6. Spoon the soap into your molds and smooth the top.
7. Allow the soap to harden overnight and then remove from the mold. Cut into desired soap bars.

#3 Calming Chamomile Soap

Chamomile is a wonderful relaxing agent. Not only does it help to calm the body, but it is a wonderful skin moisturizer that helps fight skin blemishes and soothe irritated skin.

Ingredients:

- ☐ 15 ounces Coconut Oil
- ☐ 15 ounces Olive Oil
- ☐ 12 ounces Almond Oil
- ☐ 6 ounces Shea Butter
- ☐ 1.5 ounces Castor Oil
- ☐ 15 ounces Distilled Water
- ☐ 7.2 ounces Sodium Hydroxide Lye
- ☐ Chamomile Flowers
- ☐ 1 part Pine Essential Oil
- ☐ 1 part Orange Essential Oil
- ☐ ½ part Lavender Essential Oil

Directions:

1. Start by infusing the Chamomile flowers in a jar by pouring boiled water on them and allowing them to steep until the water is cool. Strain out the liquid, and you'll have a wonderful Chamomile tea to use in your soap.
2. While the tea is cooling, get your oils melted in the crock pot with the heat on low.
3. Carefully add your lye to the water and gently stir until fully dissolved. Allow the lye solution to cool for a little bit.
4. Pour the lye solution into the oils.
5. Stir the mixture until you achieve a thick trace that is the consistency of pudding.
6. Cover the crockpot and allow the soap to cook. Once the soap is the consistency of mashed potatoes, it is finished.
7. Add your essential oils at the end after the crock pot is turned off and the soap has sat for a few minutes.
8. Pour your soap into your desired mold and allow to cool.
9. Remove from mold and cut into desired bars.

#4 Acne Fighter with Tea Tree and Orange

This is a wonderful bar soap for those suffering from acne breakouts. You can use this soap recipe without worrying about drying out your skin. The oils in this soap help heal your skin while also moisturizing and toning your skin.

Ingredients:

- ☐ 7.8 ounces Olive Oil
- ☐ 6.5 ounces Lard
- ☐ 5 ounces Coconut Oil
- ☐ 1.5 ounces Avocado Butter
- ☐ 1.5 ounces Castor Oil

- ☐ 1-ounce Beeswax
- ☐ 1-ounce Grapeseed Oil
- ☐ 1 ounce Canola Oil
- ☐ 8.35 ounces Distilled Water
- ☐ 3.35 ounces Sodium Hydroxide Lye
- ☐ 2 teaspoon Bentonite Clay
- ☐ 1 ounce Tea Tree Essential Oil
- ☐ 0.5 ounce Orange Essential Oil

Directions:

1. Start by making your lye solution. Carefully add the lye to water and stir until completely dissolved. Set aside to cool.
2. Melt your oils and butter in a crockpot on low heat.
3. Add the lye solution to the crock pot and stir until a thick trace is achieved, the consistency of pudding.
4. Place the lid and cook for about an hour or until it achieves the consistency of mashed potatoes. If it climbs the sides of the crockpot remove from heat and stir.
5. Once finished, turn off the crockpot and allow to sit for a few minutes before stirring in your clay and essential oils.
6. Scoop into your desired mold and smooth the top.
7. Allow to cool overnight and then cut into desired bars.

#5 CELLULITE ERASER

Everyone has experienced cellulite at some point, and it can be rather difficult to deal with. The ingredients in this soap will help to reduce the appearance of cellulite while also exfoliating your skin and leave a wonderful scent behind.

Ingredients:

- 15 ounces Distilled Water
- 7.2 ounces Sodium Hydroxide Lye
- 15 ounces Olive Oil
- 15 ounces Coconut Oil
- 12 ounces Sweet Almond Oil
- 6 ounces Shea Butter
- 1 tablespoon Ground Coffee
- 1 ounce Rosemary Essential Oil
- 1-ounce Grapefruit Essential Oil
- ½ ounce Cedarwood Essential Oil
- ½ ounce Patchouli Essential Oil
- 1 tablespoon French Pink Clay

Directions:

1. Start by turning your crock pot on low and adding your oils and butter so they can start melting.
2. Prepare your lye solution by adding the lye to the water carefully and then gently stirring until completely dissolved. Set aside to cool.
3. After the oils are melted, pour the lye solution into the crock pot.
4. Add your French Pink Clay.
5. Blend and mix the soap until thick trace is achieved, the consistency of pudding.
6. Replace the lid on the crockpot and allow to cook. If you notice it rising the sides remove from heat and stir down well.
7. Once the soap is finished, it will be the consistency of mashed potatoes. Turn off the heat and allow to cool a few minutes before completely stirring in the essential oils.

8. Spoon the soap into your desired mold and pack it down before smoothing the top.
9. Allow to cool in the mold overnight.
10. Remove from the mold and cut into desired bars.

#6 Dry Skin Relief

If you've ever had dry skin or sensitive skin you know how hard it can be to find a soap that keeps you hydrated for long periods of time. This basic soap is free of fragrances and preservatives, so it is good for sensitive skin while also providing plenty of moisture to relieve dry skin.

Ingredients:

- ☐ 2.9 ounces Almond Oil
- ☐ 2.9 ounces Cocoa Butter
- ☐ 2.9 ounces Coconut Oil
- ☐ 4.4 ounces Olive Oil
- ☐ 14 ounces Rice Bran Oil
- ☐ 2.6 ounces Shea Butter
- ☐ 3.9 ounces Sodium Hydroxide Lye
- ☐ 9.6 ounces Distilled Water

Directions:

1. Start by preparing your lye solution. Carefully add lye to the water and gently stir until fully dissolved.
2. Melt your oils in the crock pot on low heat.
3. Combine both when they are about 110 degrees Fahrenheit by pouring the lye solution into the crockpot of oils.
4. Stir the soap until a thick trace is achieved. It will have the consistency

of pudding.
5. Cook until the soap is the consistency of mashed potatoes.
6. Spoon into your desired mold and allow to set for 24 hours.
7. Remove from the mold and cut into desired bars.

#7 Soothing Aloe Vera

Aloe Vera is a wonderful soap ingredient that offers many benefits for the skin. It is a simple recipe that creates a rejuvenating bar.

Ingredients:
- ☐ 14.9 ounces Coconut Oil
- ☐ 13.4 ounces Olive Oil
- ☐ 10.5 ounces Lard
- ☐ 2.5 ounces Shea Butter
- ☐ 9.6 ounces Aloe Gel
- ☐ 6.7 ounces Sodium Hydroxide Lye
- ☐ 9.9 ounces Distilled Water

Directions:

1. Start by carefully adding lye to the water and gently stirring in until completely dissolved. Set aside to cool.
2. Place the oils in your crockpot on low and allow to melt.
3. When both the lye and oils are about the same temperature, carefully pour the lye solution into the crockpot of oils.
4. Add the aloe vera gel and stir until you achieve trace or the consistency of pudding.
5. Cook until finished when the soap is the consistency of mashed potatoes.
6. Spoon into the desired mold and allow to cool 24 to 48 hours.

7. Remove from mold and cut into desired bars.

#8 BASTILLE HONEY SKIN SOAP

This soap is ideal for babies and those with sensitive skin. It also features the warm and calming scents of vanilla and lavender for a truly wonderful bar of soap to help your skin.

Ingredients:

- ☐ 9.3 ounces Distilled Water
- ☐ 3.54 ounces Sodium Hydroxide Lye
- ☐ 21 ounces Olive Oil
- ☐ 4.5 ounces Shea Butter
- ☐ 2.5 ounces Castor Oil
- ☐ 1 tablespoon Honey
- ☐ 1.5 ounces Lavender Essential Oil
- ☐ 0.5-ounce Vanilla Extract

Directions:

1. Place your oils in the crock pot on low to start melting.
2. Carefully pour the lye into the water and mix until fully dissolved.
3. Gently pour the lye into the melted oils.
4. Mix under trace is achieved, it will be the consistency of pudding.
5. Cook until finished, it will be the consistency of mashed potatoes.
6. Firmly press into the soap mold of your choice.
7. Allow cooling overnight.
8. Remove from the mold and cut into desired bars.

#9 Rose Infused Balancing Soap

Rose is a wonderful ingredient in a skin care soap. The rose helps to balance the natural pH level of the skin. Which helps control excess oil while soothing and moisturizing the skin.

Ingredients:

- ☐ 4.17 ounces Sodium Hydroxide Lye
- ☐ 9 ounces Rose Tea
- ☐ 15 ounces Herb Infused Oil
- ☐ 8 ounces Coconut Oil
- ☐ 2.5 ounces Castor Oil
- ☐ 4.5 ounces Sweet Almond Oil

Directions:

1. Slowly but carefully add the lye to the cooled herbal tea and stir until fully dissolved. Allow cooling.
2. While the lye is cooling, add your oils to the crockpot on low heat.
3. Once both mixtures are at 100 degrees Fahrenheit, you can pour the lye mixture into the melted oils.
4. Stir until trace is achieved, it will look like pudding.
5. Cover and cook until finished, it will look like mashed potatoes.
6. Scoop into your desired molds and allow to cool for 24 hours.
7. Remove from mold and cut into desired bars.

#10 Sensitive Skin Bar

The Calendula flower is great for making a sensitive skin bar. It will soothe irritation and reduce skin rashes.

Ingredients:

- ☐ 4.17 ounces Sodium Hydroxide Lye
- ☐ 9 ounces Calendula Tea
- ☐ 15 ounces Herb Infused Oil
- ☐ 8 ounces Coconut Oil
- ☐ 2.5 ounces Castor Oil
- ☐ 4.5 ounces Sweet Almond Oil

Directions:

1. Carefully add your lye to the Calendula Herbal Tea and stir until fully dissolved.
2. Place your oils in your crockpot on low heat to melt.
3. Once both the oils and lye reach 100 degrees Fahrenheit you can pour the lye into the oils.
4. Stir the soap until trace is achieved, it will resemble pudding.
5. Cover and cook until it resembles mashed potatoes.
6. Spoon into your desired molds and allow to cool overnight.
7. Remove from mold and cut into desired bars.

MELT AND POUR SOAP RECIPES

FLORAL SCENTED SOAPS

#1 Rose Soap

Rose has always been a popular additive in beauty products because of its elegant floral scent. This simple melt and pour recipe allows you to create a Vitamin C rich soap that smells wonderful.

Ingredients:

- ☐ 32 ounces white melt and pour soap base
- ☐ 4 teaspoons Rose Clay
- ☐ 2 teaspoons Rosehip Powder
- ☐ 2 tablespoons Poppy Seeds
- ☐ 0.3 ounce Lavender Essential Oil
- ☐ 0.3-ounce Lemongrass Essential Oil

Directions:

1. Prepare your colors by mixing the Rose Clay with 1 tablespoon of 99% isopropyl alcohol and the Rosehip Powder with 1 tablespoon of 99% isopropyl alcohol.
2. Chop the soap base into small uniform pieces and place in a large heat-safe bowl. Melt the soap in the microwave in 30-second bursts. In between, stir the soap to help it melt evenly and prevent overheating. Continue this process until completely melted.
3. All in the clay and powder to the melted soap and stir until completely mixed.
4. Add in the essential oils and poppy seeds, stirring to mix fully.

5. Check the temperature of the soap, wait until it is about 125 degrees Fahrenheit and then pour into your desired mold.
6. Spray the top with 99% isopropyl alcohol to remove air bubbles and allow the soap to harden anywhere from four hours to overnight.
7. Remove from the mold and cut into bars.

#2 Lavender Honey Soap

Two of the best ingredients in soap is the skin nourishing benefits of honey and the calming, relaxing scent of lavender.

Ingredients:

- ☐ 1 pound Honey Soap Base
- ☐ 10 to 15 drops Lavender Essential Oil

Directions:

1. Slice the soap base into cubes and put in a heat-safe microwave bowl.
2. Microwave in 30-second bursts and stir in between until fully melted.
3. Add the essential oil and stir until well mixed.
4. Pour into your desired mold.
5. Allow to sit undisturbed until cool, about 30 to 90 minutes.
6. Remove from the mold and cut into desired bars.

#3 Square Carnations

Carnations are an elegant and fragrant flower. This simple recipe gives you a beautiful, elegant appearance and wonderful fragrance without a lot of effort.

Ingredients:

- ☐ 32 ounces Shea Melt and Pour Base
- ☐ 32 ounces Aloe Melt and Pour Base
- ☐ Liquid Violet
- ☐ 2 tablespoons Lagoon Green Jojoba Beads
- ☐ 2 tablespoons Jasmine Jojoba Beads
- ☐ 2 tablespoons Sierra Sky Jojoba Beads
- ☐ 0.5-ounce Carnation Fragrance Oil

Directions:

1. Combine all of the color beads in a container and mix well.
2. Cut 16 ounces of the Shea Melt and Pour into small cubes and place in a heat safe container. Melt in the microwave in 10-second bursts, stirring between each. Once melted add in the Carnation Fragrance Oil and stir well.
3. Allow the soap to cool to between 125 to 130 degrees Fahrenheit before adding the beads, stir continually. Once cool enough add 2 tablespoons of the bead mix and stir well.
4. Pour into square soap molds, filling about a ¼ inch full. Spray with isopropyl alcohol to get rid of air bubbles and let harden for fifteen to twenty minutes.
5. Next cut up 16 ounces of Aloe Melt and Pour into cubes and prepare in the microwave as you did the first batch. Add in the Carnation Fragrance Oil and 1 teaspoon liquid violet color, stirring well.
6. After the white soap is hardened and the purple soap is 130 degrees Fahrenheit or less, then you can spray the white soap with isopropyl alcohol and pour in the purple soap on top. This should fill the mold halfway. Spray with isopropyl alcohol again to remove air bubbles.
7. Melt the rest of the Shea Melt and Pour, repeating the earlier steps to microwave and then adding 2 tablespoons of the beads and fragrance

once cool. Remember to spray the soap with isopropyl alcohol before pouring this third layer. It should now be ¾ full and spray again to remove air bubbles.
8. Melt the rest of the Aloe Melt and Pour as you did before and add the fragrance and color once cooled. Spray the isopropyl alcohol and pour the last layer and spray again to disperse air bubbles.
9. Allow the entire soap to harden for one to two hours before removing from the mold. Cut to desired bars.

#4 Rose Petal Soap

Rose is a beautiful aroma, and this soap adds a citrus note along with a warm vanilla to give you a twist on the classic favorite.

Ingredients:

- ☐ 1 pound White Melt and Pour Soap Base
- ☐ 8 ml Rose Fragrance Oil
- ☐ 2-3 tablespoons Rose Petals
- ☐ 10 drops True Red Gel Colorant

Directions:

1. Cut the soap base into cubes and place in a safe microwave bowl.
2. Microwave the base in 15-second increments, stirring between each until the base is completely melted.
3. Stir in the fragrance oil and colorant until completely mixed.
4. Add rose petals and stir until evenly distributed.
5. Pour into the desired mold and spray the top with isopropyl alcohol to prevent bubbles.
6. Allow to harden, remove from mold and cut into desired bars.

#5 Jasmine Citrus Soap

Jasmine is an elegant and graceful flower with a beautiful scent. This soap pairs that scent with the tropical fragrance of citrus.

Ingredients:
- ☐ 1 pound White Melt and Pour Base
- ☐ 9 ml Satsuma, Mandarin and Jasmine Fragrance Oil
- ☐ 8-10 drops Coral Gel Colorant

Directions:

1. Cut the soap base into cubes and place in a safe microwave bowl.
2. Microwave the base in 15-second increments, stirring between each until completely melted.
3. Stir in the fragrance oil and colorant until completely mixed.
4. Pour into the desired mold and spray the top with isopropyl alcohol to prevent bubbles.
5. Allow to harden, remove from mold and cut into desired bars.

#6 Lilac Soap

Lilacs are a beautiful and elegant flower, just like this soap.

Ingredients:
- ☐ 24-32 ounces White Melt and Pour Soap Base
- ☐ 2-5 gel colors of your choice
- ☐ 3-5 drops of color gel of your choice
- ☐ 5 drops Lilac Fragrance Oil

Directions:

1. This soap is set up to make several batches of small soaps, but you can make them in whatever size and mold you desire.
2. Cut up soap base into squares only enough for the mold you are using and place in microwave safe bowl.
3. Melt in the microwave in 15-second increments, stirring between bursts. Stir until completely mixed with no chunks.
4. Once completely melted add in the fragrance and color of your choice.
5. Pour into the desired mold and spray with isopropyl alcohol to prevent air bubbles from forming.
6. Allow to harden overnight, remove from mold.
7. Measure out enough soap for your next mold and cut into squares, place them in a microwave-safe bowl.
8. Microwave in 15-second increments, stirring between bursts. Stir until completely mixed with no chunks.
9. Add in fragrance and color of your choice. Mix well.
10. Pour into the desired mold.
11. Allow to harden overnight, remove from mold.

#7 Lemongrass and Green Tea

Green tea is a wonderful energy booster with a number of skin benefits, combine this with the beautifully refreshing scent of lemongrass, and you have a wonderful bar of soap.

Ingredients:

- ☐ 1 pound Oatmeal Soap Base
- ☐ ¼ pound Shea Soap Base
- ☐ 1 tablespoon Green Tea and Lemongrass Fragrance Oil

Directions:

1. Cut the Oatmeal Soap Base into cubes and place in a microwave-safe bowl. Microwave in 30-second intervals, stirring in between to cook evenly.
2. Stir in the fragrance oil until well combined.
3. Blend in any desired color if you want.
4. Pour your mix into your desired soap mold.
5. Next, cut up the Shea Soap Base into cubes and melt as you did the other soap base.
6. You can add a few drops fragrance oil if you want.
7. Drizzle this soap over the cooled soap that you poured into the mold.
8. Allow to cool and harden before removing from the mold.

#8 Sea Salt Jasmine

This soap allows you to have the elegant scent of Jasmine while enjoying the exfoliating of sea salt.

Ingredients:

- ☐ Crystal Clear Soap Base
- ☐ Sea Salt
- ☐ Jasmine Fragrance Oil
- ☐ Soap Colorant of your choice

Directions:

1. Cut your soap base into small cubes of any desired amount based on how much soap you plan to make. Place in a microwave-safe bowl.

2. Heat the soap in 15-second intervals, stirring between each until completely melted.
3. Add in a soap coloring of your choice, the jasmine fragrance oil at your desired strength and the sea salt. Stir until well mixed.
4. Pour into a desired soap mold and allow to cool and harden.
5. Remove from mold.

#9 Floral Garden Bar

This melt and pour soap gives you several floral scents that remind you of spring in a beautiful bar that is swirled and embedded with additional soap curls.

Ingredients:

- [ ] Clear Melt and Pour Soap Base
- [ ] Opaque White Melt and Pour Soap Base
- [ ] Soap Colorant of your choice
- [ ] 4 Vitamin E capsules
- [ ] Gardenia Fragrance Oil
- [ ] Hyacinth Fragrance Oil
- [ ] Secret Garden Fragrance Oil

Directions:

1. Cut and melt the Clear Soap Base as needed to fill your desired mold.
2. Once completely melted add in desired colorant and Hyacinth fragrance oil at the desired strength.
3. Pour into the desired mold and allow to harden.
4. Cut and melt the Opaque White Soap Base as needed to fill your desired mold.
5. Once completely melted add in desired colorant and Secret Garden

fragrance oil at the desired strength.
6. Pour into the desired mold and allow to harden.
7. Next prepare a mold big enough for six 5 ounce bars.
8. Cut curls from the first two soap batches and place in the mold while alternating colors. Spray with isopropyl alcohol between layers.
9. Melt about a cup of the Clear Soap Base as you've done before.
10. Once melted completely add in yellow color, 2 Vitamin E capsule contents, and the Secret Garden fragrance oil at the desired strength.
11. Melt about two cups of the Opaque White Soap Base and add a small amount of brown or yellow color.
12. Once melted completely add the Gardenia fragrance oil at the desired strength and the contents of the other 2 Vitamin E capsules.
13. Simultaneously pour both soaps into the mold at the same time for a swirl effect.
14. Let the mold sit until hardened.
15. Remove from mold and cut into desired bars.

#10 SUNRISE GARDEN BAR

This beautiful bar combines a wonderful floral scent with real dried flowers.

Ingredients:

- ☐ Melt and Pour Soap Base
- ☐ Soap Colorant of your choice
- ☐ Vitamin E Capsules
- ☐ Secret Garden Fragrance Oil
- ☐ Hyacinth Fragrance Oil
- ☐ Dried Calendula Petals
- ☐ Dried Chamomile Flowers

- ☐ Ground Annatto

Directions:

1. Melt enough Clear Soap Base for your molds.
2. Once completely melted add coloring of your choice and Hyacinth fragrance oil.
3. Pour into your mold and allow to harden.
4. Melt enough Opaque White Soap Base for another mold.
5. Once completely melted add coloring of your choice and Secret Garden fragrance oil.
6. Pour into your mold and allow to harden.
7. Cut curls from these two soaps and place in a rectangular soap mold while alternating color. Spray isopropyl alcohol between layers.
8. Melt one cup of White Melt and Pour Soap Base.
9. Once completely melted add in a small handful of your two dried flowers. Allow cooling.
10. Remelt the flower soap and pour through a strainer.
11. Add in the contents of two Vitamin E capsules and a small pinch of Annatto.
12. Allow to cool a few minutes and then pour into the mold with curls.
13. Allow cooling and harden. Remove from mold and cut into desired bars.

13.

UNIQUE SOAPS

#1 Lemon Poppy Seed

Lemon poppy seed is a popular recipe among a lot of things. I find it to be a wonderful soap scent as well. This melt and pour soap recipe is a wonderful option for those who want something unique and easy to make.

Ingredients:

- ☐ 9 ounces White Melt and Pour Soap Base
- ☐ 0.2 ounce Lemon Fragrance Oil
- ☐ ½ teaspoon Lemon Peel Powder
- ☐ ½ teaspoon Poppy Seeds

Directions:

1. Cut up the Soap Base into small cubes and place in a microwave-safe bowl.
2. Microwave in 10-15 second bursts, stirring between until completely melted.
3. Add in the fragrance oil and use a spoon to mix thoroughly.
4. Add in the poppy seed and lemon peel powder. Stir until all chunks are gone.
5. Test the temperature of the soap and pour into desired molds when it is between 125 and 130 degrees Fahrenheit.
6. After each pour, spray with isopropyl alcohol to prevent air bubbles.
7. Allow the soap to harden for two to four hours and then remove from the mold.

#2 Candy Corn Soap

Candy corn is a recognized staple whether you like to eat it or not. This is a simple layered soap with a wonderful pumpkin spice smell.

Ingredients:
- ☐ 32 ounces Clear Melt and Pour Soap Base
- ☐ 16 ounces White Melt and Pour Soap Base
- ☐ Orange Color Block
- ☐ Lemonade Color Block
- ☐ 0.6-ounce Pumpkin Spice Fragrance Oil
- ☐ 0.6-ounce Vanilla Color Stabilizer

Directions:

1. Cut the soap bases mixes into small pieces. Then place the following in three microwave safe containers:
    a. 16 ounces Clear Soap Base and 0.5 ounce White Soap Base
    b. 16 ounces Clear Soap Base and 0.5 ounce White Soap Base
    c. 15 ounces White Soap Base
2. Add a small chunk of the Lemonade Color Block to Container A and melt in the microwave in 30-second bursts. Stir between bursts to melt evenly. Once fully melted add in 0.2-ounce Pumpkin Spice Fragrance Oil and 0.2-ounce Vanilla Color Stabilizer. Stir until completely mixed and then pour into your mold. Spray the top to avoid air bubbles and allow to harden for 15 to 20 minutes.
3. Add a chunk of the Orange Color Block to Container B. Melt the soap in the microwave in 30-second bursts, stirring between each burst. Once completely melted add in 0.2-ounce Pumpkin Spice Fragrance Oil and 0.2-ounce Vanilla Color Stabilizer, stirring in completely. Check the temperature of the soap and wait until it is below 130 degrees Fahrenheit

before pouring. Be sure to spray the previous layer with alcohol first and then pour the second layer into the mold. Spray the top to prevent air bubbles. Allow to cool and harden for 15 to 20 minutes.
4. Melt the soap in Container C in 30-second bursts in the microwave, stirring between each. After completely melting, add in 0.2 ounces of Pumpkin Spice Fragrance Oil and 0.2 ounces of Vanilla Color Stabilizer and stir in fully. Again check the soap and don't pour until it is under 130 degrees Fahrenheit. Spray the layer with alcohol before pouring and then spray the layer afterward to prevent air bubbles.
5. Allow the entire soap to harden and cool for three hours or overnight. Remove from the mold and cut into triangle shapes.

#3 Honey Vanilla with Oatmeal

These are three of the best ingredients you can combine in a bar of soap. The vanilla is a warm and calming scent. The honey nourishes your skin. The oatmeal provides exfoliation and soothes the skin. This is a simple melt and pour soap with numerous benefits.

Ingredients:

- ☐ 2 pounds White Melt and Pour Soap Base
- ☐ ⅛ to ¼ cup Honey
- ☐ ¾ cup Ground Oatmeal
- ☐ 1 teaspoon Vitamin E
- ☐ 1 tablespoon Vanilla Fragrance Oil
- ☐ 1 tablespoon Frankincense and Myrrh Fragrance Oil

Directions:

1. Cut the Soap Base into chunks and place in microwave safe bowl.

2. Microwave in 15-second bursts, stirring between.
3. Once completely melted add honey and Vitamin E.
4. Allow the soap to cool for 5 to 10 minutes or until a skin starts to form.
5. Stir the skin back into the soap. Once it starts to thicken add the fragrance oils and oatmeal. Stir until completely mixed.
6. Pour into desired molds and allow to harden for several hours.
7. Remove from mold and cut into desired bars if needed.

#4 Pumpkin Spice Bars

Pumpkin spice is a popular scent around the winter seasons, but it can also be a delightful smell to enjoy year round in your soap.

Ingredients:

- ☐ 2 pounds Shea Butter Soap Base
- ☐ Red and Yellow Soap Colorant
- ☐ 2 tablespoons Pumpkin Pie Spice Fragrance Oil

Dangerous:

1. Cut the soap base into cubes and put them in a microwave-safe bowl.
2. Melt the soap base in the microwave in 20 to 30-second increments, stirring between each interval until completely melted.
3. Stir in the fragrance oil and a few drops of the red and yellow soap colorant. Use fewer drops for a subtle color and more drops for a vibrant color.
4. Pour the soap into your desired molds and allow to cool for about 30 minutes.
5. Remove from molds.

#5 Peaches and Cream Soap

When I think of fruit, I always go to peaches and cream. This is a wonderful fruity scent with a calming vanilla side. Perfect for a delicate bar of soap.

Ingredients:

- ☐ 1 pound Goat's Milk Soap Base
- ☐ Peach Soap Colorant
- ☐ Peach Fragrance Oil

Directions:

1. Cut your soap base into cubes and place in a microwave-safe bowl.
2. Melt in the microwave in 20 to 30-second intervals, stirring between each until completely melted.
3. Add about 10 drops of both the colorant and the fragrance oil.
4. Pour into your desired molds and allow to cool for 30 to 90 minutes.
5. Remove from mold and cut into desired bars if needed.

#6 GROUND COFFEE SOAP

Coffee is a wonderful scent in soap and can be used as a refreshing bar to help you wake up in the morning.

Ingredients:

- ☐ 1 pound Melt and Pour Soap Base
- ☐ Ground Coffee Beans
- ☐ Fragrance Oil

Directions:

1. Determine exactly how much soap base you need based on your desired mold.
2. Cut your soap base into cubes and place in a microwave-safe bowl.
3. Microwave in 15-second intervals, stirring after each.
4. Add in coffee grounds until you achieve a desired mix and stir until fully mixed.
5. Add in your fragrance oil according to the desired scent.
6. Pour into your desired molds and spray with alcohol to prevent air bubbles.
7. Allow soap to harden for at least three hours.
8. Remove from mold and cut into bars if needed.

#7 Cinnamon Oatmeal Soap

Oatmeal is a wonderful ingredient to make soap moisturizing and good for the skin while the smell of cinnamon is a refreshing and enjoyable scent.

Ingredients:

- ☐ 1 pound Shea Butter Melt and Pour Soap Base
- ☐ ½ teaspoon Cinnamon
- ☐ 1 teaspoon Coconut Oil
- ☐ 4 tablespoons Ground Oats
- ☐ 5-8 drops Cinnamon Essential Oil

Directions:

1. In a small microwave-safe bowl melt the coconut oil. Add in the cinnamon and stir well.
2. Cut the soap base into cubes and place in a microwave-safe bowl. Microwave in 30-second intervals, stirring between each.

3. Allow the soap to cool a little then add the cinnamon mixture, ground oats, and essential oil. Stir well.
4. Pour your soap into desired molds.
5. Allow soap to cool overnight. Remove from mold and cut into bars if needed.

#8 Vanilla Cinnamon Soap

This is similar to the last soap but doesn't contain the oatmeal. It is a wonderfully smelling soap to use year round.

Ingredients:

- ☐ 1 pound Olive Oil Melt and Pour Soap Base
- ☐ 6 ml Cinnamon Essential Oil
- ☐ 1-2 tablespoons Vanilla Bean Specks
- ☐ 8 Cinnamon Sticks

Directions:

1. Cut your soap base into cubes and place in a microwave-safe bowl.
2. Microwave the soap base in 15-second intervals, stirring between each until completely melted.
3. Stir in the essential oil until completely mixed.
4. Pour soap into desired molds.
5. Sprinkle with vanilla bean specks.
6. Press a cinnamon stick into each soap bar if desired.
7. Allow hardening overnight.
8. Remove from the mold and cut into bars if needed.

#9 Citrus Soap

Citrus soap is great for those who want a vibrant smelling and colorful looking soap.

Ingredients:

- ☐ Shea Butter Melt and Pour Soap Base
- ☐ Lemon, Grapefruit and Orange Essential Oils
- ☐ Lemon Peel

Directions:

1. First cut up your soap base into cubes, using as much as you need to fill your desired soap molds.
2. Place the cubes in a microwave-safe bowl and microwave in 30-second intervals, stirring between each.
3. Once the soap base is completely melted, add in 10 drops each of your essential oils and stir completely.
4. Sprinkle the lemon peel in the bottom of your desired molds.
5. Pour your soap mixture into the molds.
6. Allow to harden overnight and then remove from molds.

#10 Tropical Soap

There is something about a wonderfully smelling tropical soap bar that allows you to be transported to an exotic destination. To make this even better, I try to find a soap mold that allows me to make a tropical looking soap along with the scent.

Ingredients:

- ☐ 1 pound Soap Base
- ☐ Green Mica
- ☐ Pink Mica
- ☐ 1 teaspoon tropical fragrance oil of your choice

Directions:

1. Cut your desired soap base into cubes with enough to fill your desired molds.
2. Place in microwave-safe bowl and microwave in 30-second intervals, stirring between.
3. Once completely melted, add in the mica and fragrance, stirring well.
4. Pour into desired molds.
5. Allow soap to harden overnight.
6. Remove from molds and cut if needed.

6.

MEDICATED SOAPS

#1 Lavender and Oatmeal Soother

Oatmeal is a wonderful skin soother that can help moisten and nourish your skin. The lavender also has calming effects on the mind and body.

Ingredients:

- ☐ 9-10 ounces of Goat Milk Melt and Pour Soap Base
- ☐ 1 tablespoon Dried Lavender Flowers
- ☐ ¼ cup Quick Cook Oats
- ☐ ¼ teaspoon Lavender Essential Oil

Directions:

1. Cut the soap base into chunks and add the oats and lavender.
2. Microwave in 30-second intervals, stirring between intervals until fully melted.
3. Add in the essential oil and mix completely.
4. Pour into desired soap molds.
5. Allow hardening overnight.
6. Remove from molds and cut into bars if needed.

#2 Turmeric Soap

Turmeric has numerous benefits for the body inside and out, making it a wonderful addition to soap. Turmeric is a great anti-inflammatory and can help revitalize the skin.

Ingredients:

- ☐ 60 ounces Goat Milk Melt and Pour Soap Base
- ☐ 2 teaspoon Turmeric Powder
- ☐ 0.8 ounce Orange Essential Oil

Directions:

1. Cut the soap base into cubes and place in a microwave-safe container.
2. Melt in the microwave in 30-second bursts, stirring between each one until completely melted.
3. Mix the Turmeric Powder into 2 tablespoons of isopropyl alcohol.
4. Once the soap is melted, add in the Turmeric Powder and the essential oil. Mix thoroughly.
5. Pour the soap into desired molds and spray with isopropyl alcohol to prevent air bubbles.
6. Allow the soap to harden overnight.
7. Remove from the mold and cut into bars if needed.

#3 PURE CHARCOAL SOAP

Charcoal is a wonderful skin purifier. It will help remove all the impurities from your skin, leaving your skin looking younger.

Ingredients:

- ☐ 32 ounces Aloe Vera Melt and Pour Soap Base
- ☐ 2 teaspoons Activated Charcoal
- ☐ 0.8 ounce Tea Tree Essential Oil

Directions:

1. Cut the Melt and Pour Soap Base into cubes and place them in a microwave-safe bowl.
2. Melt the soap base in the microwave in 30-second bursts, stirring in between.
3. Once completely melted, mix in the activated charcoal with 2 tablespoons of isopropyl alcohol. Stir until there are no clumps.
4. Add in the essential oil and stir to combine completely. Wait for the soap to cool to under 130 degrees Fahrenheit then pour into the desired mold.
5. Spray the top of the soap with isopropyl alcohol to prevent any bubbles from forming.
6. Allow the soap to harden overnight.
7. Remove from the mold and cut into bars if needed.

#4 Coffee and Cream Soap

Coffee has wonderful benefits for skin, it cleanses and tones the skin; while also smelling great. The ingredients in this soap also help moisturize the skin as well.

Ingredients:

- ☐ 8 ounces Coconut Opaque Melt and Pour Soap Base
- ☐ 2 teaspoons Lanolin
- ☐ 2 teaspoons Aloe Vera Gel
- ☐ 3 teaspoons Coffee Grounds
- ☐ 2 teaspoons Heavy Whipping Cream
- ☐ 10 drops Coffee Fragrance Oil
- ☐ 10 drops Vanilla Fragrance Oil

Directions:

1. Cut your soap base into cubes and place in a microwave-safe bowl.
2. Microwave in 30-second bursts, stirring in between.
3. Once completely melted, add all the other ingredients and stir until completely mixed.
4. Pour into desired molds.
5. Allow hardening overnight.
6. Remove from molds and cut into bars if needed.

#5 Citrus Antibacterial Soap

Citrus not only smells refreshing and clean, but many of the essential oils in this soap also have antibacterial properties to help your skin stay healthy.

Ingredients:

- ❏ 2 pounds Shea Butter Soap Base
- ❏ 8-10 drops On Guard Essential Oil
- ❏ 8-10 drops Lemon Essential Oil

Directions:

1. Cut your soap base into cubes and measure out how much you'll need for your desired mold.
2. Place in a microwave-safe bowl and microwave in 30-second increments, stirring in between until completely melted.
3. Add in the essential oils. You can choose to add in yellow soap colorant if you want.
4. Pour the soap into your desired mold.
5. Allow hardening overnight.
6. Remove from mold and cut into bars if needed.

#6 Chest Decongestant

Every cold season you find yourself getting congested and sick. Give yourself a fighting chance with these cubes. They are quick and easy to make, plus they help decongest your chest and get you through the cold season.

Ingredients:

- ☐ 4 ounces Coconut Oil
- ☐ 4 ounces Raw Shea Butter
- ☐ 4 ounces Beeswax Pellets
- ☐ 10-15 drops Eucalyptus Essential Oil

Directions:

1. Melt your coconut oil, shea butter and beeswax in a microwave-safe bowl. Microwave at 10-second intervals, stirring between each.
2. Once completely melted, mix in the essential oils.
3. Pour into your desired mold.
4. Allow hardening overnight.
5. Remove them from the mold and use as needed.

#7 Soothing Oatmeal Soap

Nothing is more soothing and nourishing to the irritated skin than oatmeal. This soap offers nothing but simple oatmeal to soothe even the most irritated skin.

Ingredients:

- ☐ 8 ounces White/Opaque Melt and Pour Soap Base
- ☐ 8 ounces Clear Melt and Pour Soap Base

- ☐ ½ ounce Oatmeal

Directions:
1. Cut your soap bases into cubes and melt in the microwave. Microwave in 15-second bursts, stirring in between each.
2. Grind your oatmeal in a coffee grinder.
3. Combine the two soap bases.
4. Add in any fragrance oil if you desire or leave plain for those with skin sensitivities.
5. Add the oatmeal and stir until evenly combined.
6. Pour the soap into your desired molds.
7. Spray with alcohol to prevent air bubbles from forming.
8. Allow hardening overnight.
9. Remove from molds and cut into bars if needed.

#8 Triple Butter, Charcoal and Clay Bar

This soap bar is a great all around bar that works for nearly any type of skin condition. You have a triple butter base to help moisturize and soothe skin. The charcoal helps to exfoliate and cleanse the skin of any impurities. The clay in the bar helps to purify and tone your skin, giving it a radiant glow.

Ingredients:
- ☐ 2 pounds Triple Butter Crystal Melt and Pour Soap Base
- ☐ 2 tablespoons Activated Charcoal Powder
- ☐ 2 tablespoons White Kaolin Clay
- ☐ 20 ml Palmarosa Essential Oil

Directions:

1. Cut your soap base into cubes based on the amount needed for your molds.
2. Place the cubes in a microwave-safe bowl and heat in 30-second increments, stirring in between until completely melted.
3. Add in the charcoal and clay, stirring until well combined.
4. Add in the essential oil and stir to distribute.
5. Pour the soap into your desired molds.
6. Allow the soap to harden overnight.
7. Remove from molds and cut into bars if needed.

#9 CUCUMBER, AVOCADO, AND OATS

This is a wonderful and unique soap. The cucumber gives a refreshing scent. The oats help to soothe the skin. The avocado help reduce inflammation and heal dry skin.

Ingredients:

- ☐ Avocado Oil Melt and Pour Soap Base
- ☐ ¼ cup Oats
- ☐ Cucumber Melon Fragrance

Directions:

1. Cut the desired amount of soap base into cubes and place in microwave safe container.
2. Microwave at 10-second intervals, stirring between each until completely melted.
3. Add the oatmeal and desired level of fragrance, stirring until well combined.
4. Pour soap into desired molds.

5. Allow cooling overnight.
6. Remove from molds and cut into bars if needed.

#10 Charcoal and Peppermint

This soap is another one with the benefits of charcoal, but also includes the refreshing scent of peppermint.

Ingredients:

- ☐ 2 pounds Goat Milk Melt and Pour Soap Base
- ☐ ¼ to ½ pound Shea Butter Melt and Pour Soap Base
- ☐ 1-2 tablespoons Activated Charcoal
- ☐ ½ to 1 teaspoon Peppermint Essential Oil

Directions:

1. Start by first melting down the Goat Milk Soap Base. Cut it into cubes and heat in the microwave at 10-second intervals, mixing between each until completely melted.
2. Stir in the essential oil based on your scent preference.
3. Stir in the charcoal to completely mix.
4. Pour the mixture into your desired soap molds.
5. Melt the Shea Butter Soap Base as you did the Goat Milk.
6. Pour a small amount of this soap into the charcoal soap. Using a wood skewer, swirl the Shea Butter soap around the charcoal soap to create a marbled appearance.
7. Allow the soap to harden overnight.
8. Remove from molds and cut into bars if needed.

GLYCERIN, LIQUID & GOAT MILK SOAPS

GLYCERIN SOAP RECIPES

#1 Apple Soap

A clear soap with the scent of sweet and fresh apples is a wonderful soap to have on hand for the whole family.

Ingredients:

- ☐ 4 ounces clear, unscented glycerin soap base
- ☐ 1 tablespoon liquid soap
- ☐ 1 teaspoon liquid glycerin
- ☐ ½ teaspoon apple fragrance oil
- ☐ 2 drops red food color
- ☐ ½ teaspoon ground cinnamon

Directions:

1. Melt the soap base in the microwave.
2. Add the liquid soap and glycerin, stirring gently and until fully mixed.
3. Add fragrance, color, and cinnamon. Stir well.
4. Let stand for a few minutes to thicken.
5. Stir once more to evenly distribute the cinnamon.
6. Pour into desired molds.
7. Allow hardening overnight.
8. Remove from molds.

#2 Apricot Soap

This is a wonderful fruit soap; the apricot is a mild and pleasant scent that leaves you feeling refreshed.

Ingredients:

- ☐ 1 pound White Glycerin Soap Base
- ☐ 12 drops Canary Yellow Color
- ☐ 11 drops Red Color
- ☐ 1 teaspoon Apricot Fragrance Oil

Directions:

1. Melt the soap base in the microwave.
2. Once completely melted, add color and fragrance.
3. Pour into desired soap molds.
4. Allow hardening overnight.
5. Remove from molds and cut into bars if needed.

#3 CANDY CANE SOAP

One thing that comes to mind with a candy cane is a unique and colorful swirl. That is what you get to enjoy with this simple glycerin soap.

Ingredients:

- ☐ ½ pound Opaque Glycerin Melt and Pour Soap Base
- ☐ 1 teaspoon Stearic Acid
- ☐ Red Colorant
- ☐ Candy Cane Fragrance Oil

Directions:

1. Melt the soap base and stearic acid separately.
2. Combine both when completely melted and whisk well.
3. Add the fragrance oil to the desired scent.
4. Pour into desired molds.
5. Dip the tip of a toothpick in the red colorant and then swirl in the soap to marbleize.
6. Allow hardening overnight.
7. Remove from molds.

#4 Cherry Cheesecake

This is a truly unique and wonderful soap to make. The tart and crisp scent of cherry mixed with a calming vanilla scent.

Ingredients:

- ☐ 1 ½ pounds White Glycerin Melt and Pour Soap Base
- ☐ ½ pound Clear Glycerin Melt and Pour Soap Base
- ☐ 2 ½ teaspoon Oatmeal, Milk, and Honey Fragrance
- ☐ 1 teaspoon Vanilla
- ☐ 1 tablespoon Cherry Fragrance
- ☐ Dash of Lemon Fragrance
- ☐ Red Colorant
- ☐ Green Colorant
- ☐ Yellow Colorant
- ☐ 1-2 tablespoons Finely Ground Oatmeal

Directions:

1. Melt ½ pound of the white soap base.
2. After completely melting add as much coloring as needed to make a dark

red. Add 2 teaspoon of cherry fragrance.
3. Pour into the desired mold, allow to cool then remove from mold and set aside.
4. Melt 4 ounces of the clear soap base.
5. After completely melting add 2 drops of green coloring and red coloring. Add ¾ teaspoon of the Oatmeal, Milk and Honey Fragrance Oil. Mix in the oatmeal. Pour evenly into two springform pans.
6. Melt one pound of white base.
7. After completely melted add a few drops of yellow coloring. Add 1 ¾ teaspoon of Oatmeal, Milk and Honey Fragrance Oil, vanilla and lemon fragrance.
8. Spray the mix already in the springform pans with alcohol and add this layer on top, evenly in both pans leaving about ¼ to ½ inch headroom.
9. Allow cooling until fairly solid.
10. Spray the cake top with alcohol and arrange the soaps from the first mix as desired.
11. Melt 4 ounces of the clear base.
12. When completely melted, add red colorant to make deep red and add 1 teaspoon of cherry fragrance. Spoon over the red soaps and allowing excess to flow around them.
13. Allow cooling about 30 minutes and you are done.

#5 Chocolate Soap

Who doesn't love the scent of chocolate? It is invigorating and pleasant. This is a simple melt and pour glycerin soap with a wonderful scent.

Ingredients:

- ☐ 12 ounces Grated Glycerin Soap

- ☐ 5 ounces Distilled Water
- ☐ ¼ cup Instant Cocoa Powder
- ☐ ⅛ ounce Chocolate Fragrance Oil

Directions:

1. Combine the grated soap and water in a saucepan and set on medium heat.
2. Once the soap is melted, add the cocoa powder and fragrance oil.
3. Stir well. Pour into desired molds.
4. Allow hardening. Remove from molds.

#6 CITRONELLA SOAP

Citronella not only has the benefit of repelling insects, but it can also be a wonderfully scented soap. Great for those summer days and nights.

Ingredients:

- ☐ 1 cup Grated Glycerin Soap
- ☐ ½ cup Distilled Water
- ☐ 10 drops Citronella Essential Oil
- ☐ 5 drops Eucalyptus Essential Oil
- ☐ 1 tablespoon Dried and Crushed Pennyroyal Leaves

Directions:

1. Melt the soap and water either in a saucepan on medium heat or in the microwave.
2. Mix in the ingredients and whip until it doubles in volume.
3. Spoon the soap into the desired molds or make into balls with your

hands.
4. Allow to harden and remove from molds.

#7 Coffee and Cream

Personally, I love the smell of coffee and love having the scent of it in my soap to help get me going in the morning. Consider making this simple soap for yourself.

Ingredients:

- ☐ 4 ounces Glycerin Melt and Pour Soap Base
- ☐ 1 teaspoon Ground Espresso
- ☐ 1 teaspoon Powdered Milk
- ☐ 10 drops Coffee Fragrance Oil

Directions:

1. Melt the soap in a small saucepan over low heat.
2. Remove from heat once completely melted and stir in the ingredients.
3. Once well mixed, pour into desired molds.
4. Allow hardening for three hours then remove from molds.

#8 Rosemary and Cream

This is a twist on the standard fruits and cream. It gives you the pleasant scent of rosemary mixed with the warm scent of vanilla. A unique and wonderful combination.

Ingredients:

- ☐ 1 pound Glycerin Melt and Pour Soap Base

- ☐ 1 cup Whole Milk
- ☐ ½ teaspoon Rosemary Essential Oil

Directions:

1. Melt the soap base in the microwave as instructed.
2. Once completely melted, add in the milk and essential oil.
3. Stir until completely mixed then pour into your desired molds.
4. Allow hardening for a couple of hours then remove from mold and cut into bars if needed.

#9 Cinnamon Soap

Cinnamon is a truly wonderful scent that makes for an excellent and fragrant soap.

Ingredients:

- ☐ 4 ounces Glycerin Melt and Pour Soap Base
- ☐ 10 drops Cinnamon Oil

Directions:

1. Melt the soap base as instructed.
2. Stir in the cinnamon oil and mix well.
3. Pour into desired molds.
4. Allow to hard for three hours then remove from molds.

#10 Aloe Vera and Nettle

This soap doesn't have much scent, but is wonderful for a variety of skin conditions and can help repair your skin.

Ingredients:

- ☐ 1 cup Glycerin Soap Base
- ☐ ⅛ cup Aloe Vera Gel
- ☐ 2 tablespoons Dried and Crushed Nettle Leaf

Directions:

1. Melt the soap base as instructed.
2. Add additional ingredients and stir well.
3. Pour into desired molds.
4. Allow hardening overnight.
5. Remove from molds and cut into bars if needed.

LIQUID SOAP RECIPES

#1 Liquid Castile Soap

Ingredients:

- ☐ 24 ounces Olive Oil
- ☐ 16 ounces Coconut Oil
- ☐ 9.35 ounces Potassium Hydroxide Lye Flakes
- ☐ 32 ounces Distilled Water
- ☐ 10 to 12 cups Distilled Water

Directions:

1. Add the Olive Oil and Coconut Oil to a large crockpot and turn on high.
2. While the oils are melting, place your 32 ounces of Distilled Water into a medium stainless steel bowl.
3. Carefully add the lye to the water and stir to dissolve.
4. Once the oils are warm and melted, carefully add the lye solution into the crockpot.
5. Blend the oils and lye with an immersion blender. Blend immediately for five minutes or until the mixture begins to thicken. Cook for the next 30 minutes while blending every 5 minutes.
6. Once the soap is too thick to blend, place the lid on the crockpot and leave to cook on high for three hours.
7. Return every 30 minutes to fold and stir the soap with a spatula or wooden spoon.
8. After three hours, test the soap. Measure out an ounce of soap and add 4 ounces of boiling or very hot water. Stir gently until the soap is

dissolved. Allow it to cool, if it is opaque or if oils float to the surface then continue cooking for another hour and retest. Otherwise, if it is clear, then you can proceed.
9. Add 10 cups of distilled water to the crockpot. Break up the soap as best as possible.
10. Place the lid on the crockpot and turn to warm for 8 hours to overnight and stir when you can.
11. After 8 hours, if you notice chunks of soap or a thick skin forming, then you should add another cup to two of distilled water.
12. Once the soap is fully dissolved with no chunks, then you can ladle your soap into desired containers.

#2 Liquid Dish Soap

Ingredients:

- ☐ 1 ½ cups Boiling Water
- ☐ ¼ cup Grated Bar Soap
- ☐ ¼ cup Liquid Castile Soap
- ☐ 2 ¼ teaspoon - 1 tablespoon Super Washing Soda
- ☐ ½ teaspoon Glycerin
- ☐ 15-40 drops Essential Oil Fragrance of your choice.

Directions:

1. Boil water on the stove over medium/high heat. Add in the grated bar soap and stir until completely dissolved.
2. Remove from heat and pour into the desired container.
3. Add the liquid castile soap, 2 ¼ teaspoons super washing soda and glycerin. Stir thoroughly.

4. Allow the soap to sit overnight with occasional stirring. If you need it thicker, then warm it up and dissolve in another ¾ teaspoon washing soda and allow it to sit overnight again.
5. If the soap is clumpy, place it in the blender or mix with an immersion blender.
6. After you get the right consistency, then you can mix in desired essential oils.
7. Place in a disperser container of your choice, and you're good to go.

#3 MOISTURIZING CREAM HAND SOAP

Ingredients:

- ☐ 0.26 ounce Castor Oil
- ☐ 0.07 ounce Jojoba Oil
- ☐ 0.35 ounce Olive Oil
- ☐ 0.17 ounce Shea Butter
- ☐ 1-ounce Coconut Oil
- ☐ 0.7 ounce Palm Oil
- ☐ 3.17 ounces Stearic Acid
- ☐ 1.8 ounces Glycerin
- ☐ 0.17-ounce Sodium Hydroxide Lye
- ☐ 0.89-ounce Potassium Hydroxide Lye
- ☐ 3.23 ounces Distilled Water
- ☐ 0.08-ounce Melted Stearic Acid
- ☐ 0.13-ounce Glycerin Mixed with the Stearic Acid
- ☐ 3.23 ounces Aloe Juice or Water
- ☐ 0.88 ounce Aloe Juice
- ☐ 0.16-ounce Allantoin
- ☐ 0.08-ounce Kaolin Clay

- ☐ 0.16-ounce Hydrolyzed Silk
- ☐ 0.16 ounce Goat's Milk Powder

Directions:

1. Preheat the oven to 250 degrees Fahrenheit.
2. Place oils/ butter and first glycerin measure in a soap pot and heat until just melted.
3. Add both lyes to the water measure and set aside to cool.
4. Add the lye water to the oils/ butter/glycerin mix and stick blend until smooth and uniform.
5. Allow the soap to rest for a few minutes.
6. Cover the pot and place in the oven for 45 minutes to an hour.
7. Check every 15 minutes and stir.
8. Heat the stearic acid and glycerin blend until melted and add to the hot soap.
9. Turn off the oven and leave the pot covered overnight.
10. Whip the soap until it loosens.
11. Use a stick blender and alternate between adding the aloe juice and blending until you achieve the consistency of frosting.
12. Add additives and stir by hand.
13. Transfer to a glass or ceramic dish with a lid. Cover and cure for a minimum of two weeks.
14. Test the texture and whip the soap. If it is too think you can add extra aloe juice ¼ teaspoon at a time.
15. Add color and scent as desired.
16. Pour into the desired dispenser.

#4 LIQUID BODY WASH

Ingredients:

- ☐ 8 ounces of your preferred bar soap
- ☐ 2 tablespoons Glycerin
- ☐ 1 gallon of water

Directions:

1. Grate the bar soap and place in a stock pot with the water and glycerin.
2. Heat on medium heat until the soap is completely dissolved.
3. Remove from the heat and allow to cool for 10-12 hours.
4. Beat with a hand mixer and add water as needed to get the desired consistency.
5. Add any fragrance you desire.
6. Funnel into your desired container.

#5 FOAMING LIQUID SOAP

Ingredients:

- ☐ 245 ml Liquid Castile Soap Base
- ☐ 5 ml Vitamin E
- ☐ 10 drops Eucalyptus Lemon Essential Oil
- ☐ 10 drops Lavender Essential Oil

Directions:

1. To use in a traditional pump or flip-top bottle simply combine ingredients, seal and agitate to combine.
2. To use in an airless foamer combine the ingredients and then dilute with water in a 1:3-6 ratio until you have a thin and watery liquid. Agitate to

mix thoroughly. Pour into your bottle and seal.

#6 Charcoal Facial Cleanser

Ingredients:

- [ ] 0.5 ounce Cocoa Butter
- [ ] 0.25 ounce Shea Butter
- [ ] 3.5 ounces Liquid Castile Soap
- [ ] 1 teaspoon Liquid Soy Lecithin
- [ ] 2 ml Rosehip Seed Oil
- [ ] 15 drops Birch Tar Essential Oil
- [ ] 15 drops Rose Absolute Blend
- [ ] 5 drops Vitamin E
- [ ] 5 drops Rosemary Extract
- [ ] 1 teaspoon Activated Charcoal Powder

Directions:

1. Melt the Cocoa Butter and Shea Butters in a double boiler.
2. Stir the Soy Lecithin into the melted butter until thoroughly combined.
3. Gently stir in the Castile Soap.
4. Stir in the Rosehip Seed Oil.
5. Stir in the essential oils, Vitamin E and Rosemary Extract.
6. Whisk in the Activated Charcoal Powder.
7. Pour into a glass bottle with a lotion pump and allow to cool completely before using.

#7 Honey and Dandelion Floral Liquid Soap

Ingredients:

- ☐ 8 ounces Coconut Oil
- ☐ 4 ounces Olive Oil infused with Dandelion
- ☐ 4 ounces Sunflower Oil
- ☐ 4 ounces Castor Oil
- ☐ 4.63 ounces Potassium Hydroxide Lye
- ☐ 13.75 ounces Dandelion Tea or Distilled Water
- ☐ 1 teaspoon honey mixed with 1 teaspoon warm water
- ☐ Vegetable Glycerin
- ☐ Distilled Water

Directions:

1. The first step is to prepare your Dandelion Tea. Place 1 cup of Dandelion Flowers in a heatproof jar and pour 1.5 cups of hot distilled water over them. Allow the tea to infuse for 20 to 30 minutes then strain. Cool completely before using in the soap recipe.
2. Place the cooled tea in a stainless steel or heatproof container. Add more distilled water if needed.
3. Add the lye to the dandelion tea and stir well. Set the lye solution aside.
4. In a slow cooker combine the oils and turn the heat on low. Add in the dandelion tea and lye solution. Hand stir for about 5 minutes until well mixed.
5. Start blending with a stick blender until you achieve trace.
6. Stir in honey and water mixture.
7. Cover the slow cooker and keep on low heat. Check the soap every 30 minutes or so and stirring each time.
8. Continue cooking about 2 hours until you have a Vaseline consistency.
9. Weigh your soap paste and multiply the weight by 0.20 to get the amount of glycerin needed, then multiply the weight by 0.80 to get how much Distilled Water you need.

10. Combine the glycerin and water in a deep saucepan and bring to a boil. Scrape the soap paste into the mixture then cover the pan and turn off the heat, leaving the pot on the burner.
11. Allow the mixture to come to room temperature, stirring and mashing occasionally.
12. Bring the mixture back to a boil once or twice and allow to cool again, stirring to break up large lumps.
13. Keep the soap in a covered stainless steel pan for a few days, occasionally stirring until all of the soap paste is dissolved.
14. Pour into jars and allow to settle for a few more days.

#8 Lavender and Oatmeal Body Wash

Ingredients:

- ☐ 3 cups Distilled Water
- ☐ ¼ cup Oatmeal
- ☐ ¼ cup Liquid Castile Soap
- ☐ 6-12 drops Lavender Essential Oil
- ☐ 1 teaspoon Vitamin E Oil
- ☐ 2 teaspoon Jojoba or Avocado Oil

Directions:

1. Bring the water to a boil. Pour the boiling water over the oatmeal in a glass bowl. Allow to sit for one to two hours and then strain to remove the oats from the water. Discard the oats and set the water aside.
2. Mix the castile soap, essential oil, Vitamin E and jojoba/avocado oil in a small bowl with a whisk until completely mixed.
3. Pour enough of the soap/oil mixture to fill 10-15% of a foaming soap dispenser.

4. Pour the oatmeal water into the dispenser until almost full, and you're ready to go.

#9 Moisturizing Soap

Ingredients:

- 1 cup of Liquid Castile Soap in the prefered scent
- 1 cup Distilled Water
- 3 tablespoons Coconut Oil

Directions:

1. Pour the liquid soap into a glass bowl and then add the water.
2. Add in the coconut oil and mix everything by stirring.
3. Transfer to a dispenser to use.

#10 Liquid Laundry Soap

Ingredients:

- 1 cup very hot water
- 1 cup castile soap, the scent of your choice
- ½ cup washing soda
- ½ cup borax

Directions:

1. Place the borax and washing soda in a small pitcher.
2. Add the hot water and stir until fully dissolved.
3. Pour into the desired container and add castile soap.
4. Cap container and tilt back and forth to mix.

5. Add cold water until container is full, leaving room to mix.
6. Cap the container again and tilt back and forth to mix.
7. Allow cooling, occasionally shaking to blend.

GOAT MILK SOAP

Goat milk isn't that difficult to work with in soapmaking. It only requires a little extra effort and knowledge of temperatures. The process for making goat milk soap is the same, so I'm going to give a general guideline for making goat milk soap and then include a few recipes for you to try.

THE PROCESS

The main issue when working with goat milk is that you don't want the mixture to get too hot otherwise the natural sugars in milk will burn, turn the soap a light-amber color with a foul odor. While these will go away, you won't be able to have a white bar of soap.

The key is to pour the milk into ice cube trays the day before making your soap. It is best to work with frozen or slushy milk during the lye making process in order to keep temperatures down while mixing. Use a thermometer during the process and keep a close eye on it. If the temperature gets over 100 degrees Fahrenheit, you should stop and allow the mixture cool down before continuing. Another option is to place the entire bowl in an ice bath of help keep temperatures down during the process. Once you've successfully mixed your lye with the milk, set it aside and move on to your oils.

Don't overheat the oils, just enough to blend them. Turn off the heat and allow the oils to cool to 80 to 90 degrees Fahrenheit or less. Once the lye solution is at the same temperature or less, slowly pour the lye into the oils. Stir by hand at first, until the texture and color are even. Then use a stick blender and mix completely until a light trace is achieved. Then add your essential oils and mix some more.

Once the soap thickens, you can pour into molds. Place the mold in the freezer the moment you're finished to prevent the soap from going to the gel stage. After 24 hours, remove from the mold and cure for six to eight weeks in a ventilated area.

Now let's look at some recipes.

#1 Oatmeal and Honey

Ingredients:

- ☐ 5.3 ounces Apricot Kernel Oil
- ☐ 8.8 ounces Coconut Oil
- ☐ 11.5 ounces Olive Oil Pomace
- ☐ 2.5 ounces Cocoa Butter
- ☐ 7 ounces Palm Oil
- ☐ 4.9-ounce Sodium Hydroxide Lye
- ☐ 11.6 ounces Goat Milk
- ☐ 2 ounces Oatmeal, Milk and Honey Fragrance Oil
- ☐ 3 teaspoons Titanium Dioxide

#2 Rosemary and Peppermint

Ingredients:

- ☐ 8.32 ounces Lard
- ☐ 4.64 ounces Coconut Oil
- ☐ 2.08 ounces Shea Butter
- ☐ 0.96 ounces Castor Oil

- ☐ 6.08 ounces Goat Milk
- ☐ 2.245 ounces Sodium Hydroxide Lye
- ☐ 0.4 ounce Rosemary Essential Oil
- ☐ 0.4 ounce Peppermint Essential Oil

#3 Avocado and Dill

Ingredients:

- ☐ 12 ounces Lard
- ☐ 1.5 pounds Coconut Oil
- ☐ 1.5 pounds Avocado Oil
- ☐ 11 ounces Distilled Water
- ☐ 10 ounces Sodium Hydroxide Lye
- ☐ 10 ounces Goat Milk
- ☐ 1 tablespoon Dill Weed finely chopped
- ☐ 1 tablespoon Anise Essential Oil
- ☐ 3 tablespoons Fennel Essential Oil
- ☐ 1 ½ teaspoons Grapefruit Seed Extract

#4 Milk and Honey

Ingredients:

- ☐ 8 ounces Goat's Milk Soap Base
- ☐ 2 tablespoons Honey
- ☐ 5-10 drops Orange Essential Oil
- ☐ Optional fresh herbs of your choice

#5 Rosemary

Ingredients:

- ☐ 4 ounces Goat Milk Glycerin
- ☐ ¼ teaspoon Ground Rosemary
- ☐ Rosemary Fragrance Oil

#6 Cinnamon

Ingredients:

- ☐ 4 ounces Goat Milk Glycerin
- ☐ ¼ teaspoon Ground Cinnamon
- ☐ Cinnamon Fragrance Oil

#7 Tropical Fruit

Ingredients:

- ☐ 4 ounces Goat Milk Glycerin
- ☐ 2 drops yellow colorant
- ☐ Pinch of poppy seeds
- ☐ 2 parts Pineapple Fragrance Oil
- ☐ 1 part Coconut Fragrance Oil
- ☐ 3 parts Banana Fragrance Oil

#8 Thyme

Ingredients:

- ☐ 2 ounces Olive Oil Glycerin
- ☐ 2 ounces Goat Milk Glycerin
- ☐ 2 drops Green Colorant
- ☐ ⅛ teaspoon Dried Thyme
- ☐ Thyme Fragrance Oil

#9 Frankincense and Lavender

Ingredients:

- ☐ 1 pound Goat Milk Soap Base
- ☐ 1 teaspoon Coconut Oil
- ☐ ½ teaspoon Olive Oil
- ☐ ¼ teaspoon Almond Oil
- ☐ ¼ teaspoon Avocado Oil
- ☐ 25 drops Frankincense Essential Oil
- ☐ 25 drops Lavender Essential Oil

#10 Basic Goat Milk

Ingredients:

- ☐ 20 ounces Coconut Oil
- ☐ 20 ounces Olive Oil
- ☐ 13 ounces Lard
- ☐ 18 ounces Goat's Milk
- ☐ 9 ounces Sodium Hydroxide Lye
- ☐ 1 ounce Essential Oils or Herbs of your choice

LAST WORDS

I hope you enjoyed these recipes, I know I enjoyed making them. Once you make a few of these, I am sure that you will come up with your own unique soap recipes. The two biggest variations you can play with are scent and color. If you play with essential oils enough times you will be able to create some unique scents that no one else has.

Same goes for coloring your soaps. If you understand the color wheel like I described in my soap making book, you will be able to create some unique colors and shades again that will be uniquely yours and yours only.

They sky is the limit when it comes to being creative in soap making.

Enjoy!